The CRAFT of SONGWRITING

MUSIC, MEANING, & EMOTION

To access audio visit:
www.halleonard.com/mylibrary
"Enter Code"
1464-3856-0015-6212

SCARLET KEYS

BERKLEE PRESS

Editor in Chief: Jonathan Feist
Senior Vice President of Online Learning and Continuing Education/CEO of Berklee Online: Debbie Cavalier
Vice President of Enrollment Marketing and Management: Mike King
Vice President of Online Education: Carin Nuernberg
Editorial Assistants: Emily Jones, Eloise Kelsey, Megan Richardson
Cover Design: Ranya Karafilly

Recording Credits:

Vocals and Guitar: Hannah Siglin
Vocals and Piano: Nick Goldston, Scarlet Keys, Michelle Tobias, Sarah Walk
Audio Engineers: Nick Goldston, Andy Pinkham
Producer: Nick Goldston

ISBN 978-0-87639-192-1

1140 Boylston Street
Boston, MA 02215-3693 USA
(617) 747-2146

Visit Berklee Press Online at
www.berkleepress.com

Study music online at
online.berklee.edu

DISTRIBUTED BY

HAL•LEONARD®
7777 W. BLUEMOUND RD. P.O. BOX 13819
MILWAUKEE, WISCONSIN 53213

Visit Hal Leonard Online
www.halleonard.com

CONTENTS

ACKNOWLEDGMENTS

This book wouldn't have been possible without my incredible students whom I've had the privilege of teaching and who have also taught and inspired me.

Thank you to my patient and supportive husband Greg Lindquist during this long, arduous book-writing process, and to my amazing daughter Claire.

Special thank you to Susan Cattaneo, Steve Rochinski, Pat Pattison, Sally Taylor, Cathy Kewley, Eric Byers, Jack Perricone, Alizon Lissance, Nicky Kerr, Arnold Friedman, Jonathan Bailey Holland, Clyde Witmyer, and my esteemed colleagues Mark Simos, Jimmy Kachulis, Michael Wartofsky, and Chair Extraordinaire Bonnie Hayes.

Thanks to all my teachers, Tom Barabas, Ellen Britton, Renee-Grant-Williams, and Steve Kirby.

To my friends especially Carina Bendz, David Fogel, Pratt Bennett, Lisa Webb, Tim Hedlund, Dan Holabaugh, Paul Dolman, Nate Therrien, Shelly Kerwin, Danielle LoPresti, Rachel Heussenstamm, and Dino Cattaneo for your support and encouragement.

To my first publisher, Chuck Neese, for giving me a chance.

To my family, Beverly Keys, Charlie Keys, Mary Larson, Jenny Orten, and Betsy Halstead.

A very special thank you to Andy Pinkham for recording half of the audio samples and to the amazing Nick Goldston who sang and produced on almost every track and made the examples sound so good. Thank you to Sarah Walk and Hannah Siglin for sharing your talent on a few of the songs.

An enormous thank you to the fabulous take-no-prisoners Editor-in-Chief Jonathan Feist, for his expertise and guidance. I was so lucky to have such an amazing editor to help me through my first book.

PREFACE

When you hear a great song, you might wonder if Adele purposely decided to sing the sixth degree of the scale on that certain word to crush your soul or if Kanye West is using classical composition techniques when he writes a melody. Well, they are doing it. Maybe consciously, maybe intuitively, but either way, they are doing it and so can you. Songwriting is a craft, and craft can be learned.

Some songwriters hold onto the myth that knowing too much can somehow hurt their intuitive process and disrupt their muse. You can't know too much; you can only think too much.

Whether you study songwriting formally or not, the greatest writers are studying all the time, by listening to songs and decoding their blueprints. Like a clockmaker, you take the clock apart, you put it back together, and then you understand it so much more deeply.

Storytelling is in our bones. It's a vital part of our human experience. We share our stories because we want to be understood and to find connection. When we share our stories, we have a witness to our experience. We are entertained and inspired. We heal, and we are healed.

This book demonstrates, through examples and exercises, how each choice you make in your melody, your rhythm, your harmony, and even your song form acts as the musical body language of your stories, and how your choices can make your songs stronger.

In the following chapters, each element is discussed not only as a technique, but as a tool that will help you write the best songs you can.

I've seen these techniques transform the writing of thousands of students, as well as my own writing. Read on, I hope you find some jewels in these pages to make your songs even better.

Scarlet Keys
Boston 2018

ABOUT THE AUDIO

To access the accompanying audio, go to www.halleonard.com/mylibrary and enter the code found on the first page of this book. This will grant you instant access to every example. Examples with accompanying audio are marked with an audio icon.

PART I
Melody

Melodies are often mysterious gifts that find us on long car rides, taking a walk, in the shower, and mostly, in response to the chords that we hear or play. Melodies are found in our language. You can hear them in the patterns of our sentences and in the inflections and rhythms of our words. We intuitively know how to communicate when speaking, and much of how we communicate translates to melody writing.

Great melodies can be gifts from the gods, but there is a science behind them that can be learned. In the lessons that follow, you will dive deeply into craft and explore the characteristics of melodies found in great songs as you learn to write them too. This includes how melodic pitch, placement, rhythm, and shapes can be used to make your songs have better melodies and more emotional impact.

1

Setting Your Lyrics

So, you found a song title! You rush home and your hopeful fingers type it into your computer or scrawl it across a fresh blank page:

Never give all the heart for love

You are so excited that you jump in and write an entire song in an hour. When you finish a song, the first thing you want to do is to play it for someone. So, you drive over to your best friend's house and hold her hostage while you play her your brilliant song.

But, there's a problem. The melody is beautiful, the harmony is creative, the lyrics are fresh, but the rhythm you attached to your precious title makes the line read as:

Nev-ER give all THE heart FOR love

Instead of your captive audience of one tearing up, she's drifing off and counting ceiling tiles. Your song fell flat in the room, and you're not sure why.

If you are going to go through all of the trouble of finding a great title, it won't be as good as it could be if you put the em*PHA*sis on the wrong syl*LA*ble.

How you say *what* you say matters!

LOCATION, LOCATION, LOCATION

Lyrics are made up of stressed and unstressed syllables, and it is important to know their most effective placement in each measure of your song.

In natural speech, *pitch* is the indicator of stress. You raise your pitch on stressed syllables, and you lower it on unstressed syllables. You don't have to think about it or intend it. You learned to do this when you learned to talk.

You can write the most beautiful lyric, drench it in metaphor, and make a great recording of it. But if undeserving words or syllables are in stressed positions in the bar, your song will lose emotion and impact.

When a phrase is stressed in a way that doesn't match the natural way it would be said, it can break the spell of the song.

Where you place your lyrics in each measure is crucial to getting the most emotion out of your lyric.

How do you know which syllables to stress?

Say the word "*never*."

Now, close your eyes and listen, as you say it. Notice that it has two syllables: nev-er.

Which syllable is higher in pitch? In a two-syllable word, you will hear that your voice will go up higher on the stressed syllable and lower on the unstressed syllable. This is true of all multisyllable words.[1]

Symbol Indicator:	/		–
Word:	*Nev*	-	*er*
Rhythm:	strong		weak
Pitch:	high		low

Notice in figure 1.1 that the stronger syllable "Nev-" is set on a weaker beat, and the weaker syllable "er" is set on a stronger beat.

FIG. **1.1.** Stressed Syllable on the Weaker Beat

It sounds awkward and loses emotion. Let's place "Nev-" on the stronger beat.

FIG. **1.2.** Stressed Syllable on the Stronger Beat

Now, it feels natural, the way you would say the word in everyday conversation.

Writers often jump into writing too quickly without considering the setting of their lyrics. They may be so focused on the groove or the melody that they attach their lyric to a rhythm or melody that doesn't preserve the natural shape of the language. Often, the lyric falls out when the writer hits a chord on the piano or guitar. When the hand strums down, the lyric falls out with it.

[1] For more on multisyllable words, read Pat Pattison's book *Songwriting: Essential Guide to Lyric Form and Structure,* chapter 3 (Berklee Press, 2002).

Here is how strong beats and weak beats fall within a measure of 4/4 meter:

- Beats 1 and 3 are the strong beats.
- Beat 1 is the strongest beat.
- Beats 2 and 4 are the weak beats.

FIG. 1.3. Strong Beats and Weak Beats

All levels of 4/4 time work this way: alternating stressed and unstressed positions. Generally, odd numbers are strong and even numbers are weak. If a beat is subdivided, the odd subdivisions will be stronger than the even subdivisions. Ideally, these stressed and unstressed rhythmic positions are destined to marry stressed and unstressed syllables.

Let's go back to our title line:

Never give all the heart for love

Say the line aloud. Notice the rise and fall of the pitch, the spaces between the syllables, and how long the line is.

Now, look at the line's stressed (/) and unstressed (–) syllables:

/	–	/	/	–	/	–	/
Nev	*- er*	*give*	*all*	*the*	*heart*	*for*	*love*

...or you might hear it in triple meter:

/	–	–	/	–	/	–	/
Nev	*- er*	*give*	*all*	*the*	*heart*	*for*	*love*

If you don't take the time to match the rhythm of the line, you could end up setting it to music like this. Listen:

Audio 3

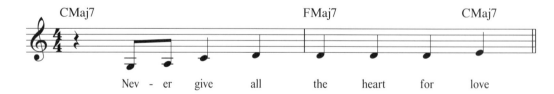

FIG. 1.4. Unmatched Stress and Rhythm

How does it feel? Did you notice that *the* has been placed on the strongest beat in measure 2? The article *the* and the preposition *for* are getting more attention than the crucial nouns *heart* and *love*.

Or, it could have been positioned like this:

FIG. 1.5. "For" Set on the Strongest Beat

Here, the preposition *for* is sitting in the strongest position. *All, the,* and *heart* are distributed equally. Notice how the line loses emotion and meaning.

FINDING YOUR MOST IMPORTANT WORDS

It's important to search your lines for the most important words before you commit them to a rhythm and melody. You want the words with the most meaning set in the stronger positions in the bar.

Emphasis is not limited to just syllables. Which word you emphasize in a line impacts the meaning. Say each of the following lines, emphasizing a different word each time. Note the emotional shift as the focus changes:

> *NEVER give all the heart for love*
>
> *Never GIVE all the heart for love*
>
> *Never give ALL the heart for love*
>
> *Never give all the HEART for love*
>
> *Never give all the heart for LOVE*

Within a lyrical line, you usually stress more than one word. But *which* words should be highlighted?

2

Parts of Speech and the Shape of Language

Language falls into two categories: meaning functions and grammatical functions. In English, when a word carries meaning, it is always stressed. We naturally stress a word that carries meaning when we speak:

<pre>
          /   /   /
  I   wish   I   had   said   I   love   you
</pre>

WORDS THAT CARRY MEANING: Adjectives, Adverbs, Verbs, Nouns

Verbs are the action words. They kick, they scorch, and they dive! They saturate the line with life.

Nouns are the stuff of life: *Cars, beer, kisses, sunsets, airport.* They give the listener specific tangible images to relate to.

Adjectives amplify and transform nouns. They color the stuff of life:

First kiss, *fragile* kiss, *dark* kiss, *awkward* kiss

Lonely airport, *empty* airport, *glistening* airport

Adverbs amplify and transform the verb:

The plane took off *quickly*, the plane took off *reluctantly*

Kiss *sweetly*, kiss *slowly*, kiss *vengefully*

Interjections express intense emotion.

Damn! Wow! She kissed me!

PARTS OF SPEECH WITH GRAMMATICAL FUNCTIONS:
Articles, Prepositions, Conjunctions, Personal Pronouns

You would only stress a grammatical function word when it carries meaning.

Pronouns identify the characters in the song. You generally put a pronoun on a strong beat when you are contrasting two pronouns:

> You're *mine* not *his*

> *I* love you, *he* doesn't

Articles specify the noun:

> I want *the* girl, not *a* girl

Conjunctions connect and contrast:

> Cake *and* ice cream, not cake *or* ice cream

Prepositions provide direction and time:

> I put the keys *on* the table, not *under* it

> I'll be there *before* you, not *after* you

Articles and conjunctions are the connective tissues that create relationships between the meaning words: verbs, nouns, adjectives, and adverbs.

ANALYZING LYRICS FOR PLACEMENT

Before you set your lyric to music, it's important to decide which words you'd like to emphasize. Let's work with the lyric *Never give all the heart for love.*

Never	*give*	*all*	the	*heart*	for	*love*
adverb	verb	adjective	article	noun	preposition	noun

FIG. 2.1. Analyzing a Lyric's Parts of Speech

What are the most important words in this line?

If the line didn't contain the word *all*, it would change everything. Of course, you give the heart for love, but *all* the heart? That's the interesting part of the line.

In this lyric, the *adjective* is really important: *all*.

It's a vital part of the meaning of the line and should be set on the strongest available beat within the measure. *Love* is also crucial and should have a stressed position. *Heart* is also important, but not as strong.

Let's see what happens when we emphasize different meaning words within the line.

FIG. 2.2. "All," "Heart," and "Love" Emphasized

In figure 2.2, *all* and *love* are placed in the most powerful positions. Think of each beat in a measure as a row of seats in a theater. Beat 1 is front row center. Both *all* and *love* deserve the best seats in the house.

Notice that *heart* is on beat 3. It's off to the right a bit in a cheaper seat, but it's still the front row. If you decided that *heart* was the most important word, you could move it to beat 1 in measure 2:

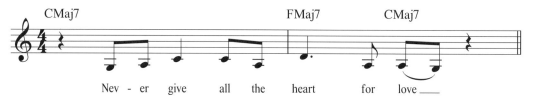

FIG. 2.3. "Heart" Emphasized

What if you want *love* sitting in the front row center stage?

FIG. 2.4. "Love" Emphasized

Now, *love* is placed on the strongest beat in the bar and highlighted further with *all* moved to beat 2.

There are many variations you could go through allowing each word in the line to move to the strong positions in the bar. The point here is to *use the strongest beats for words that hold the most meaning.*

Placed in the strong positions in the bar, they will mean what you intend them to mean. Placed badly, they will no longer mean what you meant to say.

If you want the line to feel sure and emphatic, try beginning the entire phrase on the downbeat of the first measure. It would be the same as if you leaned forward and said it with total conviction.

FIG. 2.5. Beginning on a Downbeat

You've got *never, all, heart,* and *love* in the stressed positions. It feels sure and strong because each phrase starts on the downbeat. By giving *never* the strongest stressed position in bar 1, the line becomes even more emphatic.

Let's rework the line so that the key words land on weaker beats.

Audio 9

Nev - er   give   all   the   heart   for   love.

FIG. 2.6. Key Words Deemphasized

Feels more defeated, doesn't it? Here, you'd be in the cheap seats.

Next, let's move *heart* to an unstressed position in the bar:

Audio 10

Nev - er   give   all   the   heart for   love.

FIG. 2.7. "Love" and "Heart" Deemphasized

With all of the meaning words placed on weak beats, it feels despondent. All of the phrasing is offset, still maintaining the proper relationship between stressed and unstressed syllables.

There is an inherent rhythm that comes with our language. If you bring the natural rhythm and shape of your everyday language into your songwriting, you will get more emotion out of your song.

EXERCISES

1. Set the following lyric to a melody and rhythm. Start by saying the line aloud to determine the stressed and unstressed syllables in each word. Then, place the stressed syllables in stressed positions within the bar. You can write it over one or two bars.

   Let's celebrate tonight

2. Write a melody for each of the following lines, making sure you are placing your stressed syllables in the most important positions in the bar:

   Remember California

   The love before me

   We were the lucky ones

   It was a good goodbye

3. Go through one of your finished songs, and scan your lyric for words that may have been misset. Change the rhythm or move those words within the bar so that the stressed syllables are in stressed positions in the measure.

3

Rhythmic Placement: *When* You Say *What* You Say

Imagine you are sitting in a café next to a couple. The woman leans forward and says to her boyfriend, "We've been together for six years. Do you want to marry me?"

He says, "… Yes… I want to… marry you."

She is furious. She says, "Why did you hesitate?" He says, "I *said* yes!" She says, "But you *hesitated*!" No matter how many dozens of roses he buys her or how many times he apologizes, it won't matter, because… he… hesitated. Timing is everything.

Let's translate this to songwriting. Think of phrasing as the posture of the song. He leans back in his chair and says:

FIG. 3.1. Unstable, Back-Heavy Phrasing

Don't trust this guy! That rhythmic placement is stealing the meaning. His lips said yes, but his body said no.

If he were sure he wanted to marry her, he would have leaned forward in his chair and said:

FIG. 3.2. Stable, Front-Heavy Phrasing

Now, *Yes, want,* and *marry* are on the strongest beat of the measures. Feel the difference? Ahhh, call the caterer and reserve the church!

Before you begin writing, ask yourself what action is taking place in the song. What are your characters doing? Are they leaning forward? Leaning backward? Are they hesitant? Confident? Angry? Leaving? Let your rhythmic placement reflect the emotion and posture of your characters.

So much depends on *when* you say *what* you say. When you place your lyric on the downbeat of the measure, it feels like you mean it. Starting a phrase on the first beat of a measure is referred to as *front-heavy phrasing*. When you place your lyric *after* the downbeat of the measure, it's like you are leaning back to say what you are saying and will feel more tentative. Starting your phrase after the first beat of the measure is referred to as *back-heavy phrasing*.

The following example uses back-heavy phrasing. Imagine the singer just ran into his ex unexpectedly. He knows she has a new boyfriend, but he's still in love with her, and it's hard for him to see her happy.

In a song, not every phrase needs to be all back heavy. You may vary the use of this tool on different measures depending on the content of your lyric and where you might want to highlight certain words. Here, every phrase is back-heavy to demonstrate the effect:

Audio 13

FIG. 3.3. Back-Heavy Phrasing

Audio 14

If he were happy or angry about it, his posture would be leaning in to what he was saying. Here's one option for the rhythmic interpretation of his body language using front-heavy phrasing:

FIG. 3.4. Front-Heavy Phrasing

Exercises

1. Write a song section using back-heavy phrasing in support of your lyric.

2. Write a song section using front-heavy phrasing in support of your lyric.

3. Write a song section using both front-heavy and back-heavy phrasing in support of the lyric, as needed.

4

Melodic Design

Take a moment to bring to mind your favorite song. Each section of that song is made up of melodic phrases, and each phrase has a shape to it. The melody might create a flat line [—] with the same note repeated in succession. It might move up or down by step, creating a small wave [⌒] or a gradual incline [╱] or decline [╲]. Or maybe, the melody is jagged and leaps up and down in intervals of a fourth or more [⋀⋁].

Let's look at four types of melodies:

1. **Static melody:** This is a melody built on a series of repeated notes. It is often dependent on harmony and groove and is often rhythmic.

Audio 15

FIG. 4.1. Static Melody

Songs that use static melodies:
- "Million Reasons" (Lady Gaga). Verse.
- "Shape of You" (Ed Sheeran). Verse.

2. **Step by step:** A *step melody* is a melody that moves by either half step or a whole step. It's easy to sing and easy to remember.

Audio 16

FIG. 4.2. Step Melody

Songs that use step melodies:
- "Beauty and the Beast" (Howard Ashman, Alan Menken). Verse.
- "Eleanor Rigby" (the Beatles). Verse.

3. Skip: A *skip* melody is a melody that skips a note. It moves up or down by a third.

Audio 17

FIG. 4.3. Skip Melody

Songs that use skip melodies:

- "Teenage Dream" (Katy Perry). Verse, first motif.
- "Manhattan" (Sara Bareilles). Verse, first motif.

4. Leap: This is a melody that moves to a note greater than a third away.

Audio 18

FIG. 4.4. Leap Melody

Songs that use leap melodies:

- "Wrecking Ball" (Miley Cyrus). Verse.
- "I Knew You Were Trouble" (Taylor Swift). Chorus.

Each section of a song is built using combinations of these four melody types.

5

Developing Melodies

When you have locked yourself in a dark room with nothing but a candle, a guitar, heartbreak, and writer's block, instead of someone sliding dinner underneath your door, wouldn't it be amazing if they slipped you some melodic development techniques?

The following techniques are used in formal composition and in every song that Beyoncé, Adele, and Taylor Swift have written. You can use them to build your motives and hooks.

Let's work from the classic Christmas song "Angels We Have Heard on High," and generate some new ideas based on its first motif.

1. **Repetition.** One of the most important tools is repetition. When you repeat an idea, when you repeat an idea, people remember it better. People remember it better.

Audio 19

FIG. 5.1. Repetition

2. **Melodic Sequence.** Repeat the motif, but transpose it up or down to create a new idea.

Audio 20

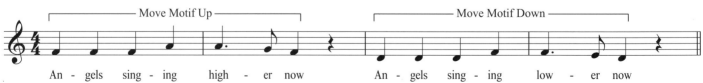

FIG. 5.2. Sequence

Audio 21

3. **Rhythmic sequence.** Keep the rhythm and change the melody.

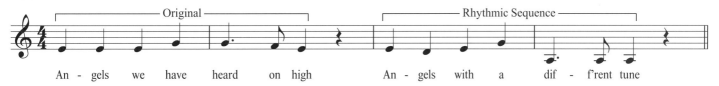

FIG. 5.3. Rhythmic Sequence

Audio 22

4. **Inversion.** Write the opposite overall shape of the melody.

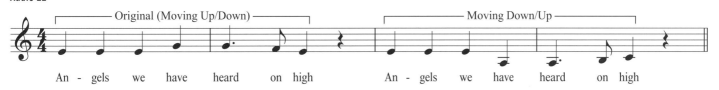

FIG. 5.4. Inversion

Audio 23

5. **Truncation.** Shorten the idea.

FIG. 5.5. Truncation

Audio 24

6. **Extension.** Make your second idea longer than the first.

FIG. 5.6. Extension

Audio 25

7. **Augmentation.** Slow the motif down by using longer note values.

FIG. 5.7. Augmentation

Audio 26

8. **Diminution.** Speed up the motif using shorter note values.

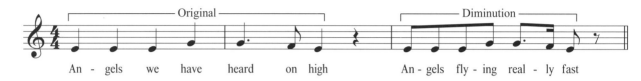

FIG. 5.8. Diminution

Audio 27

9. **Retrograde.** Let's go retro! Play your motif backwards to create a new idea.

FIG. 5.9. Retrograde

Audio 28

10. **Fragmentation.** Steal a fragment of a motif and use it to build a new idea, either repeating it exactly or as part of a melodic sequence.

FIG. 5.10. Fragmentation

Audio 29

11. **Rhythmic displacement.** Build a motive by repeating your hook, starting in a different place in the next measure.

FIG. 5.11. Rhythmic Displacement

6

Melodic Hooks

When you ask someone if they've heard a certain song, and they reply, "I'm not sure, how does it go?" what part of the song would you sing to them? It would probably be something from the chorus with a memorable hook.

Here are the five commandments of a great hook:

    I. Thou shalt be simple.

    II. Thou shalt be familiar yet different.

    III. Thou shalt be unique, and possibly contain an unexpected interval or leap.

    IV. Thou shalt contain repetition and variation.

    V. Thou shalt not repeat a melodic hook more than two times in a row without changing something even slightly when it's sung the third time.

Now, let's rework "Angels We Have Heard on High" and change the rhythms and intervals to create some interesting ideas.

Audio 30

    1. Syncopation. Write an idea that uses unexpected rhythms.

FIG. 6.1. Syncopation

Audio 31

    2. Epistrophe. Write a repeated rhythmic hook at the end of your motif to emphasize an important lyric. In the following example, the lyric focus is on "Angels."

FIG. 6.2. Epistrophe on "Angels"

Audio 32

Or, you could decide that you want to emphasize a different word and use epistrophe to bring it into focus. Let's use the word "cry" to build the motif:

FIG. 6.3. Epistrophe on "Cry, Cry, Cry"

Audio 33

3. Anaphora. Write a repeated rhythmic hook and lyric at the beginning of your motif for emphasis.

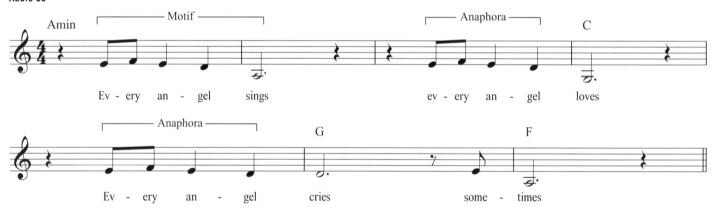

FIG. 6.4. Anaphora on "Every Angel"

4. Leap. Write a motif built on leaps.

Audio 34

FIG. 6.5. Leaps

EXERCISES

Audio 35

1. Listen to the following song in F minor with a borrowed rhythm from "Angels We Have Heard on High" (co-written with Nick Goldston). Identify and list each development technique used.

FIG. 6.6. Song Developed from the Rhythm of "Angels We Have Heard on High"

2. Find an interesting rhythmic motif from a hit song or public domain. Write an original melody to the rhythm you've found.

3. Rewrite the motif using three different melodic development techniques.

4. Pick your favorite idea, and write a verse.

5. Find another hook from a different song. Change it using these development techniques, and write a chorus section.

Answer Key to Figure 6.6

Working from the rhythmic motif from "Angels We Have Heard on High" mm. 1–2.

mm. 1–2:	Motif *a*
mm. 3–4:	Rhythmic sequence of *a*
mm. 5–6:	Rhythmic sequence of *a*, with a rhythmic variation in measure 6
mm. 7–8:	Rhythmic sequence of *a*
m. 9:	Motif *b*
m. 10:	Repetition with a rhythmic variation
m. 11:	Rhythmic sequence of *b* with a rhythmic variation
m. 12:	Fragmentation of *a*, measure 2
mm. 13–16:	Repetition of mm. 9–12
mm. 17–18:	Rhythmic sequence and variation of *a*
mm. 19–20:	Rhythmic variation of *c*
mm. 21–22:	Motif *d*
mm. 23–24:	Rhythmic sequence of *a* with variation

7

Melodic Schemes

The Rule of Three:

How many times do you think you can repeat the same idea?
How many times do you think you can repeat the same idea?
How many times do you think you can repeat the same idea?

Before your listener loses interest?

Usually, after something repeats two times, it has to change, if only slightly, on the third repetition to hold the listener's attention.

In this example (figure 7.1), everything repeats exactly. The chords change, but it needs melodic contrast.

Audio 36

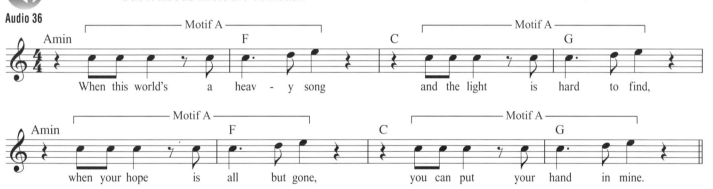

FIG. 7.1. Exact Repetition

Notice how you lost interest and wanted a change after the third measure? That's because it broke the Rule of Three.

Here is the melody scheme for the example in figure 7.1:

Lyric	Line Length	Shape of the Melody
Phrase 1: Motif A	2 bars	Ascending
Phrase 2: Motif A	2 bars	Ascending
Phrase 3: Motif A	2 bars	Ascending
Phrase 4: Motif A	2 bars	Ascending

FIG. 7.2. Melody Scheme with Repetitive Melodic Direction

Each phrase shares all the same melodic qualities:

- The number of measures for each melodic phrase
- Melodic shape
- The note values of each phrase
- Where each phrase begins and ends within each measure
- Type of melody: static, step

THE QUESTION OF CONTRAST

When you have a song that doesn't hold your interest, make note of the musical characteristics of that section, and notice if there's too much symmetry, too much repetition, or too much stability and then make changes for contrast within that section or for the next song section. You can use the chart below to check your melody.

	Length of Each Phrase	Number of Phrases	Note Durations	Shape of the Melody	Position	Type	Pitches
Verse Melody:	2 bars	4	♩. ♩ ♪	Ascending	Starts on beat 2	Static, step	C, D, E

FIG. 7.3. Melodic Characteristics

MELODIC DIRECTION

Since every phrase is moving up, let's change the melody in phrases 2 and 4 and have them move down in direction, for contrast:

Audio 37

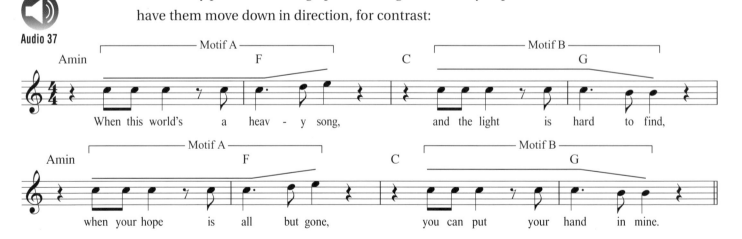

FIG. 7.4. Changing Melodic Direction for Contrast

It's better, but there is still too much symmetry. Right now, the melody scheme is:

Lyric	Line Length	Shape of the Melody
Phrase 1: Motif A	2 bars	Ascending
Phrase 2: Motif B	2 bars	Descending
Phrase 3: Motif A	2 bars	Ascending
Phrase 4: Motif B	2 bars	Descending

FIG. 7.5. Melody Scheme with Contrasting Melodic Direction

PHRASE LENGTH

Audio 38

This is a very balanced section. Let's shorten ("truncate") the last phrase and vary the melody to create more contrast.

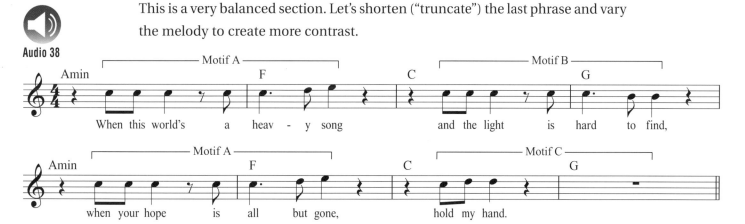

FIG. 7.6. Shortened Last Phrase

It's more interesting, and the surprise of the change on phrase 4 highlights the lyric "*hold my hand.*" Now, we've got:

Lyric	Line Length	Shape of the Melody
Phrase 1: Motif A	2 bars	Ascending
Phrase 2: Motif B	2 bars	Descending
Phrase 3: Motif A	2 bars	Ascending
Phrase 4: Motif C	1 bar	Ascending

FIG. 7.7. Melody Scheme for Shortened Last Line

LINE LENGTH

Audio 39

You could lengthen one of the lines for contrast. Let's use the tool of extension to lengthen the last line.

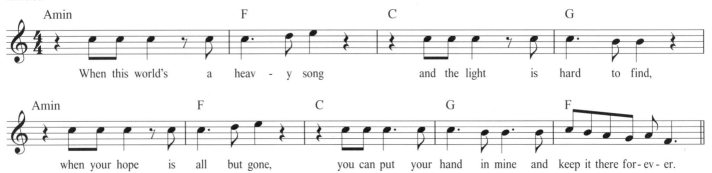

When this world's   a   heav - y   song   and the light   is   hard   to   find,

when your hope   is   all   but gone,   you can put   your hand   in mine   and   keep it there for- ev - er.

FIG. 7.8. Lengthening the Last Line

We've altered the pitch, note durations, direction of the melody, and the length of the last phrase. The result is a more interesting song section.

With this change, we are creating contrast and surprising the listener with the unexpected last line. It also supports the meaning of *forever* with the longer line. Now we've got:

Lyric	Line Length	Shape of the Melody
Line 1: Motif A	2 bars	Ascending
Line 2: Motif B	2 bars	Descending
Line 3: Motif A	2 bars	Ascending
Line 4: Motif C	3 bars	Static, then Descending

FIG. 7.9. Longer Last Line

EXERCISES

1. Write an original song section with four phrases, following the melodic scheme below.

Lyric	Line Length
Line 1: Motif A	Long
Line 2: Motif B	Short
Line 3: Motif A	Long
Line 4: Motif B	Short

FIG. 7.10. Exercise Scheme

2. Change it in two additional ways to create more contrast.

8

Melody as Tone of Voice

It's not *what* you say; it's *how* you say it that matters. Think of melody as the song's *tone of voice.* There is so much that is communicated by the way we say what we say. A question goes up in pitch; a statement goes down in pitch. A person's tone of voice tells us how they feel about what they are saying, and so does the melody of your song.

Some writers feel a loyalty to keep the first thing they write like it's gospel. But great melodies can take time to find. If you've ever heard old work tapes of John Lennon singing a line over and over again until he finds just the right melody and rhythm, you'd realize how it can pay off to take your time finding the right note for the right word. So, don't be afraid to alter the sacred chant.

Each note in a scale has its own level of emotional intensity to bring to your lyric. To find a great melody, it's important to understand the gravity of each note in the scale, as it relates to the chord. Take a look at the following C major scale. The arrows denote where each unstable scale degree wants to move to:

Audio 40

FIG. 8.1. Tonal Gravity in C Major

Unstable tones:

- The 2 wants to move down to 1.
- The 4 pulls you down to the 3.
- The 6 leans down to 5.
- The 7 is begging and dragging you up to 1 again.

Unstable pitches add so much emotion to a song. Keeping that in mind, take the following lyric line: *I'll be fine without you.*

Audio 41

When this lyric is sung with stable tones, you believe what the singer is saying. Listen to the following example:

FIG. 8.2. Melody Built on Stable Tones

Audio 42

The singer may be believable, but building melodies strictly on stable tones isn't very interesting. But what if he doesn't mean it? What if he is just trying to look strong? Pairing the important words with unstable pitches will reveal how he really feels:

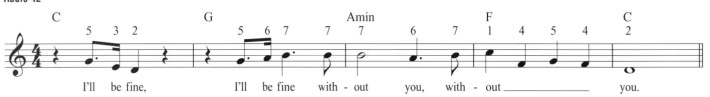

FIG. 8.3. Melody Built on Unstable Tones

In figure 8.3, the singer is saying he'll be fine, but he's singing it to a melody that's highlighting unstable tones, so we know he doesn't mean what he's saying. Tone of voice outranks meaning. His melody betrays him. Look again through this setting, and notice the other unstable tones. What mood does each note bring to the word it's paired with?

Tone of voice cues us to sarcasm, humor, doubt, confidence, flirtation, excitement, lack of excitement, surprise, hesitation, etc. As songwriters, we can model our melodic architecture after patterns of speech.

9

The Magical 6 and 7

In a major key, all of the unstable pitches (2, 4, 6, and 7) are good choices to pair with a lyric that is unstable. "Yesterday" by the Beatles creates the perfect feeling of longing with the second degree of the scale, right from the first note. Miranda Lambert supports her frustration so well in the song "Automatic" when the chorus hits using the fourth degree of the scale all through the melody. But the two rock stars of emotion in melody are the sixth and seventh scale degrees.

The 6 has a bittersweet quality to it and pulls on your heart. Adele uses this super note in her song "Someone Like You." In the song "I Can't Make You Love Me" by Bonnie Raitt, it's used in every section to rip your heart out. If you want to test this theory, rewrite both of these songs and replace the 6 with a stable note, and feel the song deflate. So much depends on the right note on the right word.

The 7 is begging to go home and creates longing. They are both powerful notes to pair with your most important lyrics.

Once these two super notes are on your radar, start to pay attention when you hear a song that makes you feel more melancholy or sad and see if it's using the 6 or the 7.

Audio 43

Listen to the following lyric paired with the stable notes 1 and 3, and a passing 2.

FIG. 9.1. Melody with 1 and 3

Audio 44

Since the words are paired with such stable notes, we believe him. He is happy that his ex found someone new. Now, listen to the same lyric changing the last two notes to the 6:

FIG. 9.2. Melody with 1 and 6

Do you believe him? No! He's not *happy*. You know how he feels by the *way* he is saying *what* he is saying. The choice of the bittersweet note really brings the emotion to that last word.

Next, listen to the last measure paired with the 7:

Audio 45

FIG. 9.3. Melody with 1 and 7

Audio 46

You don't believe him here either, do you? It feels even sadder.

Now, listen to a combination of both the 6 and the 7:

FIG. 9.4. Melody with 1, 6, and 7

Notice that *happy, found, love,* and the last syllable of a*gain* are all paired with these melodic superstars. Now, you *really* don't believe him.

In the preceding examples, the melody could have moved up to the 6 or 7 above the tonic instead of below. The effect would be even more dramatic, since a leap brings more intensity, and each measure could have contained a different chord to add even more emotion. The chords you play in conjunction to the notes you play have another layer of meaning and nuance. If they are notes that are a part of the chord or notes that are not a part of the chord (non-chord tones), it shades the meaning.

ADDING IMPACT

Unstable notes will have even more impact when they are:

- The highest note in the phrase, because it's like you are raising your voice

- Placed on a strong beat within the measure

- Placed at the beginning or the end of a phrase

- Have a longer duration than the surrounding notes

Songs that use the 6:

- "I Can't Make You Love Me" (Bonnie Raitt)
- "Into the Mystic" (Van Morrison)

A song that uses the 7:

- "Pink Moon" (Nick Drake)

A song that uses both the 6 and 7:

- "Need You Now" (Lady Antebellum)

EXERCISES

1. Write a verse with a major melody, pairing the 6 on the words where you want to bring the bittersweetness.

2. Rewrite your song section, and try replacing the 6 with the 7. Pick the best note that brings out the emotion that you want for the line.

3. Rewrite your song section using both the 6 and the 7.

Melodic Contour: Contour Narrative

For this lesson, we will explore how the shape of your melody can support the narrative.

Consider the following verse lyric:

Let down the curtains

Let down my hair

Let down my heart

Let down my heart

Before writing a melody for this lyric, take a minute to picture what's happening in the scene. The verb phrase is *let down*. *Letting down* is a descending motion, so it would make sense for the first melodic shape to also descend. The actions of letting down the curtains and letting down the hair both have descending motion:

Let down the curtains ↘

Let down my hair ↘

The direction of the melody can follow the falling curtains, and the hair falling down around their shoulders.

Which one of these actions takes the most effort to let down? The curtains, the hair, or the heart? *The heart.*

Since letting down the heart is the hardest thing to do, an ascending melody would support the struggle of the uphill battle, with the melody moving up against the heart being let down.

Audio 47

Listen to the lyric set to the following melody.

FIG. 10.1. Static

This isn't a bad melody, but it's not living up to its full potential. The shape of the melody is counterintuitive to the action taking place in the song, like using a gesture that has nothing to do with what you are saying.

You can use the shape of your melody as a contour narrative to support the action in the scene.

Now, listen to it set to a more intuitive contour:

Audio 48

FIG. 10.2. Descending, Ascending

Now, the first two lines are descending and support the action taking place in the scene. The contour of the third phrase is moving up against the content of letting down, fighting gravity. The last line goes up a whole step higher on the word *heart*, making it even harder to let down. Now, the melody is in full support of the lyric, telling a contour narrative.

EXERCISE

Write a verse and a chorus with a melody that uses contour as a narrative to support the meaning of your lyric. Keep in mind:

- Intervallic distance: static, step, skip, leap
- Melodic direction: ascending, descending
- Melodic pitches: stable, unstable
- Melodic rhythm: duration of each note

11

Intervallic Narrative

You can use a leap in your melody to create an interesting hook and emotional intensity, but you can also use the range of your intervals as a tool to offer your listener a sonic experience of distance. The further the distance between the notes in your leap, the more distance is created and if you use this to support the right words, you take your writing to a deeper level and the listener along with you.

BEGINNING LEAP

Audio 49

In the following example, the lyric tells a story about a long distance relationship, but it isn't using a leap in the melody. Take a listen.

FIG. 11.1. Without Leaps

It's not a bad melody, but choosing a melody built on small intervals isn't serving the story in support the idea of distance. Notice how the word *thousand* has an interval of only a third.

Now, listen to the next example. Each line begins with a large leap. Notice how the intervallic distance between the notes supports the lyrics' idea of *distance*. The distance between your notes can help support your story by creating sonic spatial relationships. Take a listen.

Audio 50

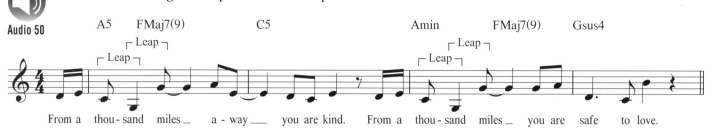

FIG. 11.2. Melody with Leaps

Now, on the word *thousand*, the notes are four notes apart. The leap creates distance and supports the lyric concept *thousand miles*. The leap back up from *thousand* to *miles* is even further—eight notes away, creating even more distance.

The second time you hear the word *thousand*, the leap again supports the lyric idea. Finally, it ends with the leap of a seventh, to support the distance with the word *love*.

Songs that use frontal leaps as a motif:

- "(Somewhere) Over the Rainbow" (Judy Garland). In the verses, there are three lines that begin with a leap melody in support of the lyric. Each intervallic hook diminishes with each motif.

- "From a Distance" (Bette Midler)

When you are casually speaking, your vocal range stays in a steady range with inflections here and there for emphasis. When you get excited, angry, or upset, your voice leaps up high to get someone's attention and to show that you are in distress. Think of the vocal range of a crying infant, a father yelling STOP when his child runs into the street, or monkeys screeching in the forest. Higher intervals bring emotional intensity and as a songwriter, you can apply this to your writing. Most chorus sections contain the highest note in the song and offer the big general emotion.

In the next example, the singer is missing someone and really upset that they are not together. Listen to the melody that follows and notice that although it's a nice melody and the singer is really good, the melody is almost a flat line built with a static and step melody and the intervals are not serving the story:

Audio 51

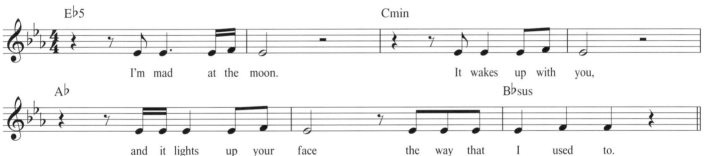

FIG. 11.3. No Leaps

Audio 52

It doesn't tell an intervallic story. In the next example, there is a leap at the beginning of each line, creating a hook and supporting the emotion of the lyric. Take a listen.

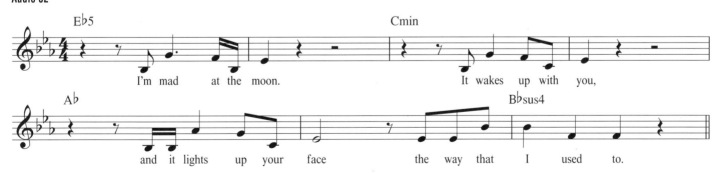

FIG. 11.4. Beginning Leap

Feel the difference? The further away the two notes are, the more intense it feels. The wide leap supports the emotion of the singer.

"Jealous" (Labrinth) includes a beginning leap.

END LEAP

Audio 53

In the next leaping melody, the leap is serving as an ending hook to each line. The technique here is that each line ends with the same rhythm, but the intervals get smaller with each line. Take a listen.

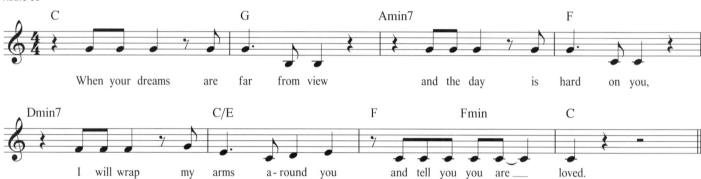

FIG. 11.5. End Leap

Watch how the intervals are supporting the changing distance:

Line 1: When your dreams are far from view (interval of a sixth)
Line 2: And the day is hard on you (interval of a fifth)
Line 3: I will wrap my arms around you (interval of a third)
Line 4: And tell you you are loved (static melody)

The intervals start as a wide-angle camera lens on the dream
Then narrows to the day
Closes in smaller to your lover's arms
Down to focus on the love and the safety of the static melody on the tonic home note

"Make You Feel Love" (Bob Dylan) includes an end leap.

INTERNAL LEAPS

You can also use a leap somewhere within a melodic line to emphasize and isolate an emotional moment. The note you leap to will have an emotional impact depending on whether it's a stable note to the key or to the chord. It will stand out even more if it's a new rhythm.

Songs with internal leaps:

- "Someone Like You" (Adele). In the verse, the melody leaps up a sixth, six measures in, when she sings the word *dreams*. The melodic rhythm changes and the word *dreams* is sung on the sixth degree of the scale with a brand-new rhythm on a non-chord tone. All of these factors add to the emotion that the large leap in the melody brings to that moment of the song.

- "Need You Now" (Lady Antebellum). This song uses internal leaps as hooks to support the emotion with a large leap of a sixth on the title lyric. Towards the end of the chorus, two more leap hooks with an interval of a sixth support the story about how the singer doesn't know how she can do without that guy she loves.

- "Friends in Low Places" (Garth Brooks). On the word *low*, in the chorus, there's a melodic leap down a fifth. It's fun to sing and makes that great song concept even better, with that unexpected leap down. That leap is used a few times to build that unforgettable hook.

EXERCISES

1. Write a four-line verse that can be supported by the use of a frontal leap as a hook. Then, write a melody for the lyric beginning each line with a leap.

2. Write a four-line verse that can be supported by an end motif that includes a leap. Repeat the line two times, each time changing the distance between the notes in the leap as it supports the meaning of the narrative. Write a fourth line that does not include the leap, but moves by step or skip, or has a static melody.

3. Write a verse with an internal isolated leap that supports the lyric in that moment of the song.

1 2

Melodic Rhythm: Acceleration and Deceleration

> *"When you use melodic rhythm in support of what is happening within the scene of your song, your listener becomes a participant."*

We are so closely linked to rhythm that people are often described as being upbeat, offbeat, or deadbeat. The rhythm of a melody can clue you into the emotional state of the singer. If melody is the song's tone of voice, think of the melodic rhythm as part of the *body language* of the song, *showing* your listener how your characters are moving and feeling.

Think of how John Williams starts off his famous minor second motif in the theme for *Jaws*. The notes speed up, and as they do, so does the shark. He used the melodic rhythm as a verb and to this day, people scream when a piece of seaweed touches their toe.

When you use melodic rhythm in support of what is happening within the scene of your song, your listener becomes a participant.

Instead of letting your melodic rhythm fall out arbitrarily conjoined to the lyric, take time to work out the rhythm of your melody. Then, you will have interesting melodies, *and* a rhythm that supports the motion and emotion of your characters. Here are two great tools you can use to help them achieve this effect.

ACCELERATION

In the following example, a guy calls his ex-girlfriend, and her new boyfriend is over at her house when she answers the call. In the verse, the pace of the melodic rhythm sounds casual and relaxed. In the prechorus section, the note values speed up to sixteenth notes, and you can feel the anxiety of the singer increase along with the accelerated rhythm. Not only is the accelerating rhythm creating contrast and momentum towards the chorus, but it also gives the listener a deeper experience of the song.

Songs that use acceleration:
- "Someone Like You" (Adele). Prechorus.
- "Teenage Dreams" (Katy Perry). Chorus.

Audio 54

FIG. 12.1. Acceleration

DECELERATION

When you establish a rhythm in one section and then slow the rhythm down in the next section, it's like driving a car and slowing down to point out something you want another passenger to pay attention to. In the following example, the verse section is made up of eighth notes and sixteenth notes. The chorus comes in with a dotted half note, and you can feel it slow down as it decelerates. This again is good contrast *and* can support the scene or the emotion of the character. The rhythm here supports the feeling of slowly reaching:

Audio 55

FIG. 12.2. Deceleration

Songs that use deceleration:

- "Chandelier" (Sia). Chorus.
- "Firework" (Katy Perry). Prechorus.

EXERCISES

1. Write a melody for a verse section using half notes, dotted quarter notes, or quarter notes.

2. Write a prechorus that speeds up rhythmically in contrast with the verse, using shorter note values.

3. Write a chorus melody that slows down in comparison, using longer note values than the prechorus.

13

Rhythmic Onomatopoeia

Beyond just being interesting and creating contrast between song sections, the rhythm of your melody can create a visceral experience for the listener.

Take the word "jump," for instance. When you say that word, its rhythm is imitating the action of the verb *jump*. Take a moment to say the word slowly. Start by saying the first consonant *j* with your teeth and jaw closed, and then open your mouth for the vowel *u*, and then close your mouth, landing on the consonant *m*, and come back up a bit with plosive *p*. You actually made your mouth *jump* by saying the word.

Much like how onomatopoeia demonstrates the sound the word makes when you say it, such as *crash*, *hiccup*, or *buzz*, your melodic rhythm can imitate the action in your song. Your melodic rhythm can act as a verb. We'll call this *rhythmic onomatopoeia*.

Say you want to write a song about being in a relationship where you want to come and go as you please. You go away but always want to come back again. To make this idea more interesting, you use the metaphor of a pendulum to support the back and forth of the relationship, since a pendulum swings back and forth. The verb in this scene is *swing*.

It would be a missed opportunity to write a melodic rhythm that is counter-intuitive to the action. Listen to the following example:

Audio 56

FIG. 13.1. "Swing" Original Melody

The rhythm doesn't give you the *experience* of swinging; the melodic rhythm and the word *swing* are not in alignment, and are counterintuitive to how the verb functions. The quarter notes stop. They don't offer a rhythmic visual of swinging, and feel more like a match for a lyric like: *wait* or *stop*.

Picture the motion of a swinging pendulum. Reach out in front of you with your eyes closed and draw that movement in the air with your arm out in front of you. Say the word *swing*. Do you say it quickly, or slowly?

When you say the word *swing*, the word starts off and swoops upward and then comes back. You can feel it in your mouth when you say it. It's not staccato; it has a long shape to it. By taking the time to say it, you can *feel the action of the word* and start to imagine a melodic rhythm taking shape that you can translate into a melody.

Listen to the next example and feel the difference:

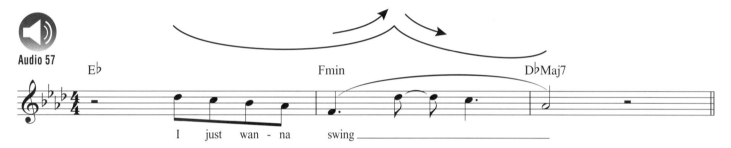

FIG. **13.2.** "Swing" New Melody (Courtesy of Liz Longley)

Here, both the direction of the melody and the rhythm of the melody pull you into the song and now *you are swinging too.* Verbs are gold; use them well.

Read the following chorus lyric:

> *Wreck me*
>
> *Wreck me*
>
> *Wreck me*
>
> *Wreck me*

Listen to it set to the following rhythm and melody:

FIG. **13.3.** "Wreck Me" Original

When you think of the word *wreck*, it's usually associated with the impact of hitting another car; you are thrust forward, then back and then forward again. It's a jarring action. In figure 13.3, the melodic rhythm is missing the opportunity to support the action taking place. This would be more suited for a scene where you were driving two miles an hour covered in bubble wrap as you slide into pile of donuts.

Now, listen to the chorus lyric set to the following rhythm:

Audio 59

Wre - e - e - eck   me,   wre - e - e - eck   me,   wre - e - e - e - eck   me.

FIG. 13.4. "Wreck Me" Onomatopoeia

Feel the wreck? Once you find your rhythm, the melody and harmony can add so much to create even more tension.

Some examples of songs that use rhythm onomatopoeia:
- "Chandelier" (Sia). Chorus.
- "Shake It Off" (Taylor Swift). Chorus.
- "Wrecking Ball" (Miley Cyrus). Chorus.

EXERCISE

1. Pick a word from the following list: ricochet, backlash, whiplash, boomerang, break, strut, machine gun.

2. Write a chorus that is four measures or longer, using the word you've chosen as a metaphor. Write a melodic rhythm that supports the action of the word.

14

Triple Meter

Most songs are written in the common meter of 4/4. Writing in triple meter using 3/4, 6/8, or 12/8 is a way to bring something fresh to your writing. This specific meter can be used to support the story you are telling and effect the listener in a way that 4/4 can't.

We'll start with the emotion typically associated with triple meter. Lullabies date as far back as 4,000 years ago from the Babylonian times, and we still sing lullabies today. Songs written in this meter are called "cradle songs" or "sleeping songs." Songs such as "Silent Night" or "Rock-a-Bye Baby" are written in 3/4. The most famous lullaby from classical music is the Brahms "Wiegenlied" (or "Cradle Song"). It's said that Brahms had sleep apnea and wrote the lullaby to help himself sleep. Lullabies are known to be soothing songs and mimic the movement a baby experiences both in the womb and while being rocked.

Let's take a look at some songs that use triple meter in support of the lyric:

- "Breathe (2 A.M.)" (Anna Nalick). The song is written in triple meter 6/8. In the story, the friend of the singer is in turmoil and is calling her friend for help. The singer offers advice using the verb *cradle*, which is supported by this time signature.

- "What the World Needs Now" (Burt Bacharach). This song is written in 3/4 supporting the lyrics when it says that the world needs *love, sweet love.*

- "Daughters" (John Mayer). This song is in 6/8. The soothing meter supports the lyric and sentiment of wanting mothers and fathers to be good to their daughters.

- "Perfect" (Ed Sheeran). This song is in 12/8 and adds to the feeling that the girl in the song is in good hands with the guy singing to her.

Triple meter is often paired with dark or sad lyrics in many country songs, folk songs, and shanties. The lyrical content of many lullabies are and were of a horrible and dark nature, because nighttime is often associated with scary and dark things. Think of the lyric "*the cradle will fall, and down will come baby, cradle and all.*"

There are many popular songs in triple meter with a dark tone. Of course, there are songs written in 3/4 with lyrics that are not dark, but regardless of content, the meter itself offers a feeling of comfort.

- "I'm So Lonesome I Could Cry" (Hank Williams)

- "Only Love Can Break Your Heart" (Neil Young)

- "Strong Enough" (Sheryl Crow) is in 3/4, and it's an interesting choice in support of the singer being in conflict but wanting to be comforted.

- "Piano Man" (Billy Joel) might feel good musically, and it supports the scene of the regulars coming into their local bar. But the singer reveals that he'd rather be somewhere else. It's almost as if Billy Joel is using the meter to soothe himself.

All of these songs have a darker story to tell. The triple meter of each song, although upsetting, soothes the singer as they sing about their pain. Regardless of how dark the content of your story or how optimistic, triple meter is soothing.

EXERCISES

1. Take one of your songs written in 4/4 time, and change the meter to either 3/4 or 6/8.

2. Pick a topic where a character in the song needs to be treated gently or is in turmoil and needs soothing. Write the song in 3/4, 6/8, or 12/8.

3. Write a lyric with a dark topic in triple meter. Keep in mind the juxtaposition of the soothing cradle feel against the negative lyric.

PART II
Harmony: The Emotional Life of Chords

It's so easy to get caught up in finding the right title, right word, or right note that harmony can sometimes be the last guy invited to the party. How often have you used the same chords you always use? Or taken a chord progression from another song and set it up with your lyrics like a blind date, without considering their compatibility?

When you play a chord, have you ever thought about the emotion it brings to your song?

In the following lessons, you have a reference guide not only to the available chords in a certain key and chords you can borrow from other keys, but you will explore what these chords have to offer your song emotionally. It would be difficult to categorically define and name the exact emotion that each chord brings to a song because emotion is subjective, but it's interesting how great writers use the same chords to create similar moods.

Play through and listen to the examples given, and then decide for yourself what you think each chord feels like to you and what it has to offer. The goal is to leave you more connected to harmony and to heighten your awareness of its emotional impact. After this section, you will handpick each chord—not because the chord is available, but because it's the exact chord you need in that exact moment of your song to make it feel just the way you want it to.

15

Primary and Secondary Chords

Let's begin with the three primary and fundamental chords in a major key: I, IV, and V. Many great songs have been written using just these three chords. They are important because these three chords state the tonality.

Let's look at what these fundamental chords have to offer:

PRIMARY CHORDS IN THE KEY OF C MAJOR		
Chords	Notes	Traits
C	C E G 1 3 5	This feels the most stable of all the chords in the key. It contains three stable tones. I is home.
F	F A C 4 6 1	This chord is in motion. It feels like it's going somewhere because it contains two unstable tones: • F wants to resolve to E. • A wants to resolve to G. • C is stable.
G	G B D 5 7 2	This is the strongest chord with the most motion because it contains the leading tone. It contains two unstable tones and one stable tone: • G is stable. • B is pulling you back home towards the tonic. • D wants to move to C.

FIG. 15.1. Primary Chords in the Key of C Major

When you listen to each chord in the context of a harmonic progression, without lyric or melody to inform it, harmony has its own story to tell.

Play the following progression in the key of C without a melody or a lyric. Notice how the movement of the chords alone contains an inherent emotional narrative.

Audio 60

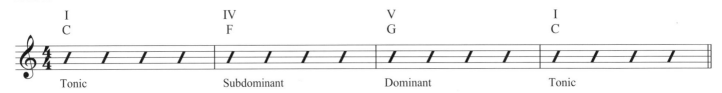

FIG. 15.2. Chord Progression: I IV V I

This progression could support any story of leaving and returning: the ups and downs of a relationship, leaving home to see the world then returning, etc. In a major key, the I chord is called the tonic, the IV chord is the subdominant, and the V is the dominant.

Melody and rhythm are crucial, but let's see what happens to a lyric when harmony is isolated from rhythm and melody.

Say the following phrase aloud:

So this is love

Without a melody to inform it, it's an ambiguous phrase. It's like tofu; it needs to be dipped in soy sauce or curry to give it flavor. You may have given it your own internal cadence as you read it, colored slightly by how you're currently feeling on the topic of love, but the words alone need music to give them context and meaning.

Here are five different progressions written to this lyric. There is a subjective interpretation for each chord change. Listen to each one and notice how the lyric shifts in nuance with each new harmonic configuration. Think about how you might interpret each harmonic narrative:

Audio 61

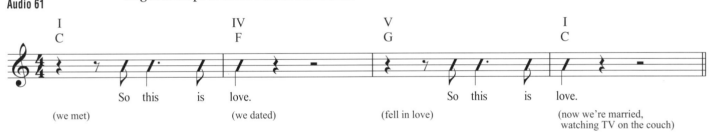

FIG. 15.3. Setting 1 with Story Analysis: I IV V I

When the I chord moves to the IV chord, notice how it's introducing something interesting that calls for your attention. When it moves to the V chord, it raises the bar of intensity and then resolves back to the home chord.

Now, listen to the setting in figure 15.4, and notice how trading places of the IV and V changes the story.

Audio 62

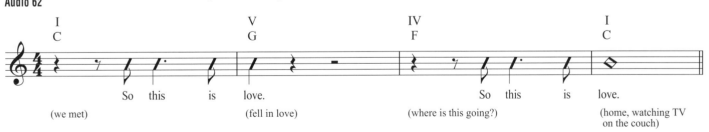

FIG. 15.4. Setting 2: I V IV I

The I chord moving to the dominant V chord is a more dramatic move than I to IV so it works well paired with the intensity of falling in love. The subtle move down to the IV chord holds your attention but is less dramatic since it's only moving down a whole step. Do you notice how there's a feeling of suspending the moment in the IV chord, which supports the question of "Where is this headed?" It feels like it's asking a question before resolving back to I. You'll often hear this cadence in church music supporting a prayer request. This *plagal cadence* holds your attention with a more subtle suspense than the V would because it contains the unstable notes 4 and 6.

Now, listen to a different harmonic order, ending the progression on something other than the tonic, and notice how it feels:

Audio 63

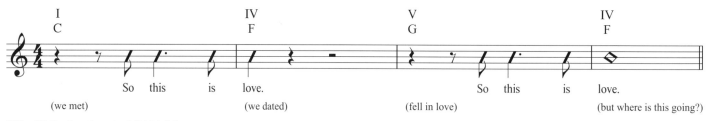

FIG. 15.5. Setting 3: I IV V IV

Again, we have the IV chord wanting to go to the I chord, but it doesn't. So we have this suspended feeling of being in love. It's in a constant state of motion, so it feels unresolved.

In the next setting, the progression is I, V, IV, then back to V.

Audio 64

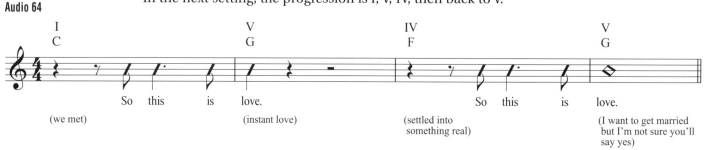

FIG. 15.6. Setting 4: I V IV V

There is such a strong pull sonically for the IV to go to the I that when it goes to the V instead, it creates even more instability and tension with no resolution.

In the next example, figure 15.7, the chords move back and forth between the I and the IV chord, creating a pattern that could be interpreted as comfort/ excitement/comfort/excitement.

Audio 65

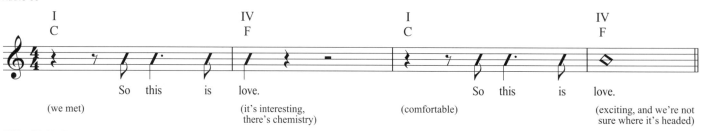

FIG. 15.7. Setting 5: I IV I IV

SECONDARY CHORDS

Now that you've explored the primary chords and the stories they tell, let's look at the secondary chords and what moods they have to offer your lyric.

Here are the secondary chords:

SECONDARY CHORDS IN THE KEY OF C MAJOR		
Chords	**Notes**	**Traits**
C Major	C E G	
D Minor	D F A 2 4 6	This chord is in motion with three unstable notes that want to resolve: • D down to C • F down to E • A down to G This chord typically moves to the V chord.
E Minor	E G B 3 5 7	Pensive/melancholy. This chord is in motion, containing one unstable note: the leading tone B up to C. It also contains two stable notes: E and G. This chord wants to move to the IV or the VI chord and sometimes to the II chord. • B up to C
F Major	F A C	
G Major	G B D	
A Minor	A C E 6 1 3	In motion with one unstable note: A, which wants to move down to G. A shade of sadness. Relative minor. Shares two stable common tones with the tonic chord, but the unstable 6 is in the root, bringing the bittersweetness as a focus. • A down to G
(B Diminished)	B D F	Rarely used.

FIG. 15.8. Secondary Chord Tendencies

16

Pedal Point

A *pedal point* is a great way to create suspense and intensity in support of a lyric. The *pedal* is a note that is played constantly while other voices move and shift above it. It is typically the tonic of the key and is holding its sonic ground while other chords move above it. A pedal creates a big, floating feeling that is unresolved, then resolved, then unresolved, and it keeps you guessing.

Let's look at the following example, first without a pedal point. This lyric doesn't feel very suspenseful. Take a listen:

Audio 66

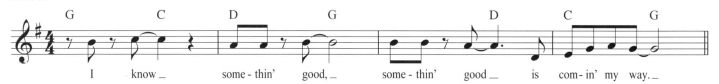

FIG. 16.1. No Pedal

Audio 67

Let's pedal the tonic note G and feel the difference:

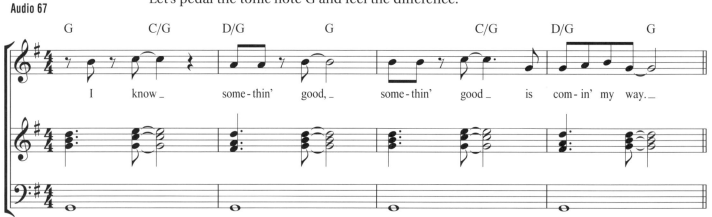

FIG. 16.2. Pedal on the Tonic G

Now, the harmony is also saying, "Something is coming." Some examples of songs that use a pedal point:

- "Change the World" (Eric Clapton). Verse.
- "Can't Stop the Feeling" (Justin Timberlake). Prechorus.

Another note that is often used as a pedal is the 5. It's a great way to cadence, so let's look at the example again, but this time, we will pedal the 5 in measures 2 and 4.

Audio 68

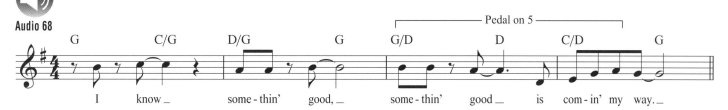

FIG. 16.3. Pedal on the 5 (D)

It's a really interesting alternative to the Vsus4 or just a plain V cadence, and it brings added suspense.

INVERTED PEDAL

Audio 69

The bass isn't the only place to use this device: you can also pedal the tonic as the highest note voiced. In this case, the pedal feels less grounding and off in the distance like something is coming but it's farther away.

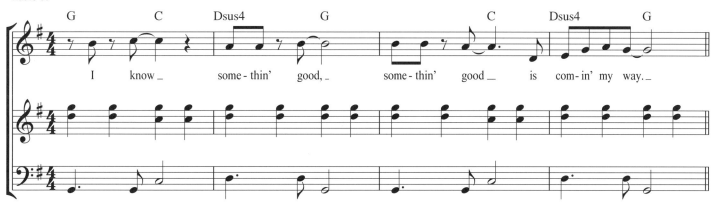

FIG. 16.4. Inverted Pedal: G on Top

An example of an inverted/high tonic pedal:

- "Say Something" (A Great Big World and Christina Aguilera). Verse.

You can also place the tonic pedal in a middle voice. There, it will still be consistent and grounding, but it will be a more subtle suspense saying, something is coming, but no rush; it will get here when it gets here. The tonic is now an internal pedal:

Audio 70

FIG. 16.5. Pedal in a Middle Voice

You can also create an entire bass figure that repeats while the chords change above it, or with it. Listen to the lyric from above with an ostinato bass:

Audio 71

FIG. 16.6. Ostinato Bass

These songs feature an ostinato bass:

- "Attention" (Charlie Puth)
- "Faith" (Ariana Grande and Stevie Wonder)

EXERCISES

1. Write a verse section using a tonic pedal.

2. Rewrite your verse, and invert the tonic to the highest voicing.

3. Move your pedal to an internal pedal.

4. Rewrite your section to cadence with the 5 as a pedal tone.

5. Rewrite your song section with an ostinato bass.

17

Substitutions for Diatonic Harmony

Think of the I chord and the IV chord as having harmonic understudies. If you want a different sound to try, there are other chords you can substitute for the primary chords.

Figure 17.1 shows you chords you can exchange for other chords in the same function category.

Tonic	Subdominant	Dominant
C Amin Emin	F Dmin	G B°

FIG. 17.1. Tonic, Subdominant, and Dominant Chords in C Major

Audio 72

Play the following progression:

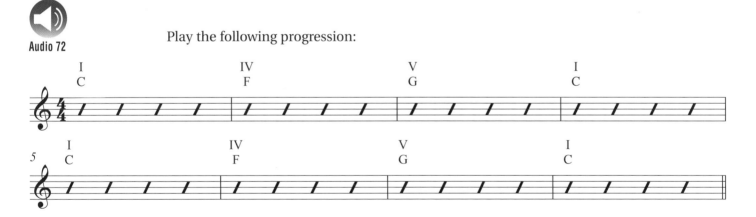

FIG. 17.2. Chord Progression with Primary Chords

Notice how the I chord isn't as interesting by the time you play it again on the second line. You can replace the I chord with another chord in the chart to create new interest and, ideally, to support the emotion of the lyric in that position.

There are two alternative tonic function chords available to substitute for the C: Amin and Emin. You won't have to change your melody to accommodate the new chord because it will function in the same way as the I chord due to the common notes they share, but it will bring its own mood to your lyric.

Audio 73

SUBSTITUTIONS FOR THE TONIC CHORD

Listen to this example of substituting the VI minor for the I chord.

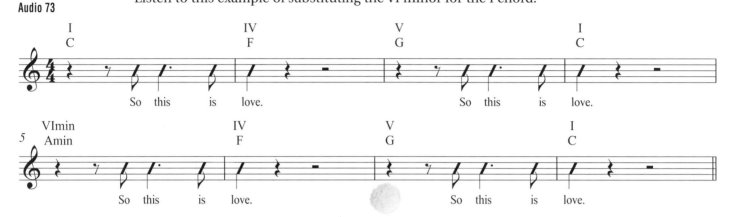

FIG. 17.3. A Minor for C

In measure 5, replacing the I chord with the VImin chord changes the way love feels the second time you hear it. Love takes a turn of sadness with the use of the A minor chord.

Now, let's substitute the IIImin chord for the I chord and see what happens.

Audio 74

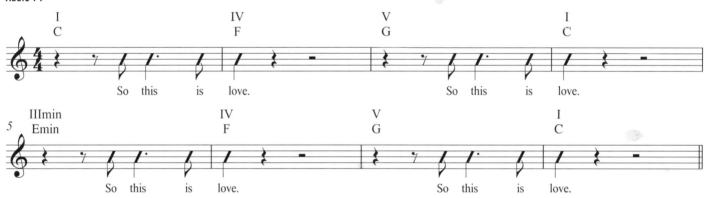

FIG. 17.4. E Minor for C

Love feels darker against the E minor chord because, while it shares two common notes with C, it has the unstable leading tone, B, which wants to move to the note C. What does it feel like to you?

SUBSTITUTION FOR THE SUBDOMINANT

Audio 75

When you want to replace the IV chord, you can use the IImin chord instead. It's a subtle move but offers a sonic change:

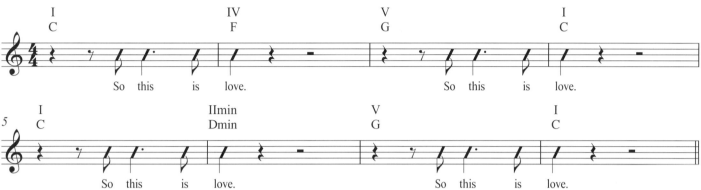

FIG. 17.5. D Minor for F

In the second measure, the C moving to the F feels bright and makes love feel great. When we substitute the II chord in measure 6 for the IV chord, notice how *love* suddenly feels warmer but moodier following the IV chord.

Let's see what happens when we move from the tonic chord to another tonic function chord in the same function family:

FIG. 17.6. Tonic Chord to Tonic Function Chord

C to E minor may feel nostalgic, melancholy, and darker. C to A minor may feel bittersweet or sad.

There really are no rules; there are only choices. If it sounds good, it *is* good. Trust your instincts and don't settle for the first chord you find. Take your time to find each chord in your progression and make sure that it is the right chord to serve each moment in your song.

18

Expanding the Palette

> "When you handpick each chord because you know what emotion it will bring to each moment of your song, your songs get better. You will begin writing intuitively and intentionally."

Up to now, we have looked at the primary chords, secondary chords, and substitution chords in relation to a I IV V progression. Each new chord will bring its own disposition or nuanced mood with it. It's important to note that a chord will feel different depending on which chord it's coming from. For this chapter, though, we will start by exploring the emotional effect of diatonic chords following the I chord.

When you handpick each chord because you *know* what emotion it will bring to each moment of your song, your songs get better. You will begin writing intuitively *and* intentionally.

We will work with two primary emotions: sad and glad. Keeping these emotions in mind, let's look at how moving from the I chord to other diatonic chords in the major key can support each feeling.

Let's work with the lyric:

I remember twenty-one.

Play a C chord. To make it feel sad, what chord would you move to next? A common move would be to go from I to VI minor, or C to A minor.

Let's listen to what the A minor brings to the lyric:

Audio 78

FIG. 18.1. C to A Minor

How does that move make twenty-one feel?

The note A is the sixth degree of the major scale, and it has a sweetness and a sadness to it all at the same time. Compared to the other chords in the key, most people would agree that it brings more sadness than the other chords.

This move occurs in:

- "All We Ever Do Is Say Goodbye" (John Mayer). Verses and chorus.
- "Brave" (Sara Bareilles). Coloring the word *outcast*.

What chord could you move to from C that would offer a deeper, more complex emotion? You were sad, but the sadness was tinged with longing or regret.

Try I to III minor, or C to E minor.

Audio 79

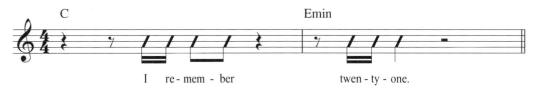

FIG. 18.2. C to E Minor

What does twenty-one feel like now?

The E minor chord brings a more complicated emotion that only the bitter-sweetness of nostalgia can. Whatever emotion you ascribe to this chord, it's the darkest chord available in the key.

Songs that use this progression include:

- "Crazy Love" (Van Morrison)
- "A Beautiful Mess" (Jason Mraz)

Let's move away from the dark side and into the simple emotion of *glad*.

Try I to II minor (C to D minor):

Audio 80

FIG. 18.3. C to D Minor

How does twenty-one feel now?

This is a perfect subtle move into a breezy contentment.

Examples include:

- "Tennessee Whiskey" (Chris Stapleton)
- "Here, There and Everywhere" (the Beatles)

Staying on a lighter note, let's turn up the volume from pleasant and content to *blessed* or *lucky*. What chord move would support this emotion?

Try I to IV (C to F):

Audio 81

FIG. 18.4. C to F

This move occurs in:

- "Brown Eyed Girl" (Van Morrison)
- "Here Comes the Sun" (the Beatles)

Try I to V (C to G):

Audio 82

FIG. 18.5. C to G

This move occurs in:

- "She Will Be Loved" (Maroon 5)
- "Let It Be" (the Beatles)

Exact feelings are subjective, but it's interesting how most people come pretty close to agreeing on how certain chords feel. The more time you spend paying attention to what feeling each chord offers, the better you will be at pairing your lyric with the best chord.

That covers it for Harmonic Emotions 101. Now, let's expand our search to include more complex chords and emotions. Let's add *mad* and *scared* to our chart. If you look up all four of the basic emotions in a thesaurus, you would find so many other nuanced choices. Keep them in mind as you expand your harmonic vocabulary.

Sad	Glad	Mad	Scared
melancholy	content	annoyed	nervous
sorry	blessed	bitter	jittery
depressed	laughing	vengeful	suspicious
grieved	ecstatic	resentful	panicked
hopeless	elated	rejected	cowardly
unworthy	joyful	outraged	shy
discouraged	resilient	disgusted	wrecked
regretful	brave	fighting	paralyzed
weeping	Manic	unforgiving	phobic

Fig. 18.6. Emotional Thesaurus

19

Stealing Chords

We've expanded our emotional choices. Now, let's expand our harmonic choices to match our deeper emotions. To do this, we are stepping outside the key to find other chords we can use. You may have heard terms like *borrowed chords* or *modal interchange*, but for this chapter, we are going to avoid those terms. We won't borrow chords; we will steal them! And *add* these outsiders to our chord palette, in a major key, to use as we would all the diatonic chords.

The first technique to finding new chords is to switch the chord qualities from what they would be ordinarily. Change the major chords to minor and the minor chords to major. Here they are in the key of C major:

Diatonic Triads:	C	Dmin	Emin	F	G	Amin	B°
Nondiatonic Triads:	Cmin	DMaj	EMaj	Fmin	Gmin	AMaj	BMaj

FIG. 19.1. Altering the Chord Quality

By adding this second row of chord choices to the palette, you can turn up the volume on the basic emotions that the diatonic chords have to offer, supporting your more intricate emotions.

Let's work with the line:

I remember twenty-one.

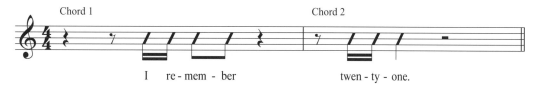

FIG. 19.2. "I Remember Twenty-One" on Two Chords

Take the example in figure 19.2, and try it out against the following chord variations:

1. I to Imin (C to Cmin). This harmonic move would arguably be the darkest move you could make. *Scared, addicted,* or *suspicious.* "Kiss from a Rose" (Seal) features this move.

2. I to IIMaj (C to DMaj). Happy elevates to *resilient, brave,* or *bold.* Two examples of this are "Forget You" (CeeLo Green) and "Lips Are Movin" (Meghan Trainor).

3. I to IIIMaj (C to EMaj). This chord demands attention and could support a feeling of *excitement, mania,* or *elevated contentment.* The following three songs use this move: "New York State of Mind" (Billy Joel), "(Sittin' On) The Dock of the Bay" (Otis Redding), and "Creep" (Radiohead).

4. I to Vmin (C to Gmin). Sadness descends into *regret* or *bittersweet nostalgia.* "Fire and Rain" (James Taylor) uses this move.

5. I to VIMaj (C to AMaj). This major chord dominates. It's bright and brings an emotion of *excitement, recklessness,* or *foolishness.* You'll find this move in the song "Crazy" (Willie Nelson).

CHORDS FROM FURTHER BEYOND THE KEY

Now, let's expand your chord palette even more by adding flatted chords. Here, we are changing the minor chords in row 1 to flat major chords, rather than just changing their chord qualities based on their diatonic roots.

Diatonic Triads:	C	Dmin	Emin	F	G	Amin	B°
Nondiatonic Triads:		DMaj	EMaj			AMaj	BMaj
Nondiatonic Flat Major Triads:		D♭Maj	E♭Maj			A♭Maj	B♭Maj

FIG. 19.3. Altering the Chord Quality. Note: C♯ and D♭ are the same chord, as are F♯ and G♭.

Why just the minor chords? Because a flat version of IV major (F major) would be E major, which we found in the previous approach. Going from I to ♭V (C to G♭) is so dissonant that it would only be used in very avant-garde music or possibly to score a film. It's not often used in popular music, so it's not included in your chart. You are always welcome to use it and see what it brings to your music, but for this lesson, we will look at chords that are used more prevalently in popular music.

By taking the chords and flatting them, they are moving down in motion, bringing the emotion with them. Let's consider each of these moves:

1. **I to ♭VII (C to B♭).** The flat-7 chord has such a special flavor to it, and it brings its own emotion of darkness. "Angel from Montgomery" (Bonnie Raitt) and "Breathe (2 A.M.)" (Anna Nalick) in the verse to support a dark feeling.

2. **I to ♭III (C to E♭).** This goes in a more assertive and moodier direction. It is often a blues/rock move, such as in the song "Hold On, I'm Coming" (Sam and Dave).

3. **I to ♭II (C to D♭).** Bright and different. This is a rare move: uplifting and strange all at the same time. This move hearkens back to the great songs of the 1940s, such as "You Stepped Out of a Dream" (Nat King Cole).

4. **I to ♭VI (C to A♭).** Another deep shade of sad. Used again in "Kiss from a Rose" (Seal).

EXERCISE

1. Take these lines from a poem by Yeats.

   Never give all the heart for love

   Will hardly seem worth thinking of

   To passionate women if it seem

   Certain, and they never dream

   That it fades out from kiss to kiss

   For everything that's lovely is

   But a brief, dreamy kind delight

   O never give the heart outright

2. Write a rhythm for the words, placing the most important lyrics in the stressed positions within each measure.

3. Harmonize the lyrics in a major key using at least three of the following chords to emotionalize the most important words: II, III, IVmin, Vmin, ♭VI, ♭VII.

You can use the following rhythm and harmony to get started. Then finish adding rhythm and harmony to the rest of the poem, or write your own rhythm.

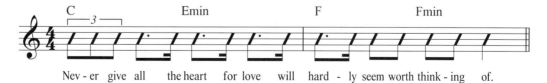

FIG. 19.4. Starting Rhythm

Seventh Chords:
Major and Dominant

Up to this point, you have been getting to know the available triads and what they have to offer a lyric. Now, let's expand the chord matrix to include seventh chords. Changing a chord from a triad to a seventh chord adds a new flavor to each chord.

This chord matrix doesn't include every possible chord; it includes the chords most often used by songwriters.

Diatonic Triads:	C	Dmin	Emin	F	G	Amin	B°
Diatonic Sevenths:	CMaj7	Dmin7	Emin7	FMaj7	G7	Amin7	Bmin7♭5
Nondiatonic Triads:	Cmin	DMaj, D♭Maj	EMaj, E♭Maj	Fmin	Gmin	AMaj, A♭Maj	BMaj, B♭Maj
Nondiatonic Sevenths:		D♭Maj7	E♭Maj7	*Fmin7*		A♭Maj7	B♭Maj7

FIG. 20.1. Seventh Chords

Let's work with the phrase:

I remember love.

Audio 83, 84

When you add the 7, it makes the chord feel warmer. Listen to the following melody, first with triads and then with seventh chords:

FIG. 20.2. Adding Major Seventh Chords to a Progression

Audio 85, 86

Listen now to a longer chord progression that includes a minor chord: first without seventh chords, and then with them.

FIG. 20.3. Adding Minor Seventh Chords to a Progression

Notice that by adding a 7 to the Amin chord in this progression, the resulting Amin7 chord feels warmer and less bittersweet.

Exercises

1. Write a verse section using only triads.

2. Add a seventh to each chord.

3. Write a chorus using two of the nondiatonic chords from the chord chart.

DOMINANT 7: THE STRONG CHORDS

Dominant 7 chords live up to their name. They are dominant! These chords are often associated with blues progressions. In a blues, you will typically see all dominant 7 chords: I7 IV7 V7 (in the key of C, they are C7 F7 G7). A good example is "Give Me One Reason" (Tracy Chapman).

Dominant 7 chords are not limited to the blues. You can turn any major triad into a dominant 7 chord and use it in a major-key progression to take advantage of its unique mood and strong pull.

You can use a dominant 7 chord unexpectedly to amplify the emotion of a single word or phrase, giving it power and strength. It's important to note that dominant chords other than the dominant V in the major key are known as secondary dominants. They are the dominant V chords of other keys and are pulling to the tonic of their key. If you use a D7 in the key of C, that chord is the dominant V chord of G. That's why it can feel so powerful in your key.

Here is a song example, set two ways. In the first progression, there are no dominant 7 chords. In the second progression, notice what the dominant 7 chords bring to the emotion of the same melody and lyric.

Audio
87, 88

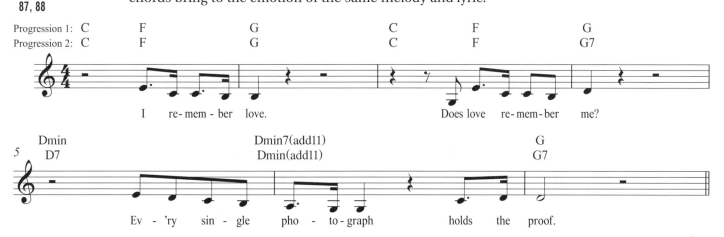

FIG. 20.4. Melody with and without Dominant 7

Hear the difference? The D7 chord demands your attention and the G7 brings a strength and dominance to that moment in the song.

Here are some songs in major keys that use the dominant 7 chord to flavor their lyrics:

- "Every Breath You Take" (the Police) is in a major key but uses the II7 chord to color the word *aches* regarding the singer's heart.
- "Man in the Mirror" (Michael Jackson) uses the II7($\sharp$9) to add intensity to the idea of changing yourself to make the world a better place.

EXERCISES

1. Play through one of the following chord progressions, noticing what emotional story is being told by the harmony.

2. Pick a progression, and write an original melody and lyric.

3. Pair the dominant 7 chords with lyrics that will convey emotions of strength, power, anger, etc.

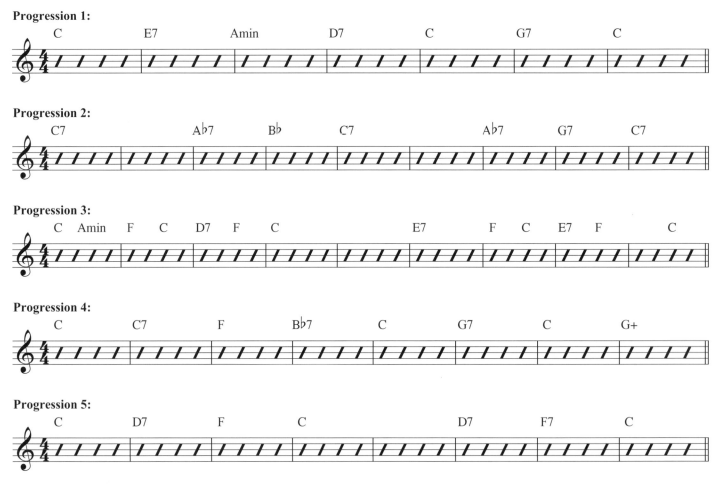

FIG. 20.5. Exercise Progressions

21

Diminished and Augmented Seventh Chords

DIMINISHED CHORDS

Diminished chords are dissonant, unstable, and lack a tonal center. Diminished chords are typically used as passing chords on their way chromatically to chords with diatonic roots, but they can also be chords you move to and stay on for a few beats up to a full measure, to really let the dissonance ring.

When you use a diminished chord in passing, it makes your listener wonder what's going to happen next. They are very intense chords—in *motion*, pulling you to the next chord.

The word "diminish" simply means "to make smaller." To find a diminished chord, you start with a minor chord and then lower the 5 down a half step.

For example, take the Cmin chord: C E♭ G. Lower the G by a half step: C E♭ G♭, to arrive at a C° chord.

Audio 89

FIG. 21.1. Cmin and C°

Diminished chords are often used as passing chords between the I chord, II chord, and III chord. They usually move to the nearest diatonic chord and make for great voice leading. Do you feel how it's pulling you forward?

Audio 90

FIG. 21.2. Diminished as Passing Chord

EXERCISE

Write a two-bar phrase with melody and lyric that uses the passing ♯II diminished chord.

DIMINISHED 7

To turn up the drama on a diminished chord, add the diminished 7. To find the diminished 7, go up a major sixth above the root note of the chord: C E♭ G♭ B𝄫 (A).

Audio 91

FIG. 21.3. C Diminished 7

Turn up the intensity by adding the 7 to the ♯I° chord: C♯°7 (C♯ E G B♭).

I to ♯I°7

Audio 92

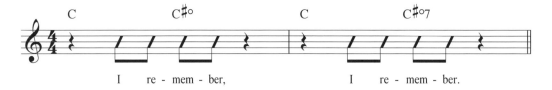

FIG. 21.4. Diminished vs. Diminished 7

What does it feel like now? By adding an additional note, you add even more suspense to the sound.

This passing diminished chord happens in countless great American twentieth-century songs:

- "Call Me Irresponsible" (Frank Sinatra)
- "For Once in My Life" (Stevie Wonder)

EXERCISES

1. Write a verse section starting on the I chord moving to the ♯I° chord in the first measure.
2. Rewrite the section using the ♯I°7 chord, and note the difference.

V to ♯V°7

Audio
93, 94

Another chord that typically moves up a half step to a sharp diminished chord is the V chord: G B D up to G♯ B D E.

Listen to the following example, first without the diminished chord, and then with it. Notice what the chord adds.

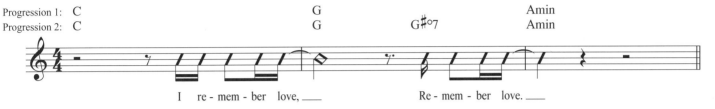

FIG. 21.5. V to ♯V°7

The passing diminished chord is waving you forward and coloring the word remember with a bittersweetness on its way to the next chord.

An example is "Living in the Moment" (Jason Mraz).

EXERCISE

Write a song section that uses the ♯V°7 chord following the V chord, supporting the meaning of your lyric.

IV to ♯IV°

Audio 95

You could also go from the IV chord up a half step to the ♯IV°. A famous example is "Everytime You Go Away" (Hall & Oates). This song uses the IV to ♯IV° from the prechorus to the chorus: F to F♯°. It pulls the listener up to the chorus.

FIG. 21.6. IV to ♯IV°

Did you feel it pulling towards a new chord?

EXERCISES

1. Write a song section that uses the sharp IV diminished chord.

2. Write a verse and then write a prechorus that uses the sharp IV diminished chord to lead into a chorus section.

DIMINISHED CHORDS THAT ARE NOT PASSING CHORDS

When you let a diminished chord have its moment in a song where it has a chance to be played for at least a full measure, the listener has more time to settle in with the sound. In this case, it really brings out the emotion of a suspended sadness in that particular moment.

I°

By following the IMaj with the I°, you are flatting two notes at once. It goes from major to dark and mysterious or a complicated sadness. You can feel it slump.

Audio 96

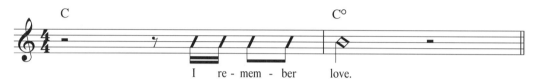

FIG. 21.7. With I° (C°)

An example is "Hate It Here" (Wilco).

EXERCISE

Write a verse section with your choice of chord progression. Within your section, use the I chord moving to the I° chord in support of your lyric.

♯V°7 (G♯°7)

Audio
97, 98

Before you listen to the ♯V°7 chord in a progression, listen to the progression first without that chord (progression 1). Notice how the diatonic V chord (G) affects the lyric. Then, we swap out the G chord for the G♯ diminished chord: G♯ B D F. What does the new chord bring to the lyric?

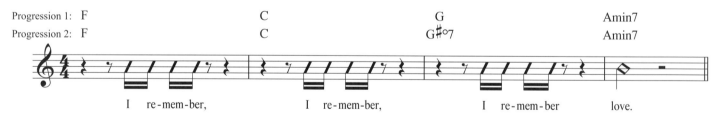

FIG. 21.8. With and Without ♯V°7

Feel the tension of the ♯V°7 chord.

EXERCISE

Write a song section using the ♯V°7 chord for a full measure within your progression in support of your lyric.

HALF DIMINISHED (or min7♭5)

The min7♭5 chord starts as a diminished triad, and you add the ♭7: C E♭ G♭ **B♭**. This is a beautiful chord to use.

Audio 99

FIG. 21.9. Cmin7♭5

You can find this in the key as you hear it, but here are two ways to use this chord that will bring the melancholy every time:

1. I to IImin7♭5 (C to Dmin7♭5): D F A♭ C. For example, "I Believe I Can Fly" (R. Kelly).

2. I to ♯IVmin7♭5 (C to F♯min7♭5: F♯ A C E). This feels brighter, and bittersweet. For example, "I'll Still Be Loving You" (Restless Heart)

Audio
100, 101

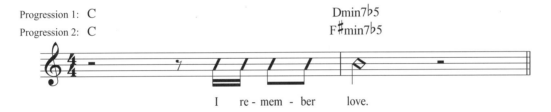

FIG. 21.10. I to IImin7♭5 and I to ♯IVmin7♭5

EXERCISE

Write a song section or change one of your existing song sections using each half-diminished move in support of the emotion of your lyric.

1. I to IImin7♭5

2. I to ♯IVmin7♭5

AUGMENTED CHORDS: YOU RAISE ME UP

What does an augmented chord bring to the party? Like the diminished chord, it brings tension, but it brings a good kind of attention: the happy kind—like if Jim Carey were a chord. It's intense, but in a good way.

The raised 5 screams, "Hey, listen up!" It's in motion, and wants to go to the next diatonic note. When you use this chord, all ears will be on that moment in your song, so make it count.

Augmented chords are great for storytelling. To augment is the opposite of to diminish. It means to make bigger. To create an augmented chord, play a major triad, and raise the 5 up a half step: C E G♯. Try augmenting these chords when you're in a major key: I, III, V, VI, and VII (in C major: C+, E+, G+, A+, and B+).

Here are three ways this chord is used:

1. Line cliché. From the I chord up to the I6 chord: C, C+, C6.

   - "For Once in My Life" (Stevie Wonder). You can feel how it's telling the story and leading to the word *love*.

2. On the III chord. III+ (or E+: E G♯ C).

   - "I Believe I Can Fly" (R. Kelly)

3. On the V chord, to turn up the power of the V+ chord going into a new section.

   - "Oh! Darling" (the Beatles)

Listen to each chord progression below, and note the effects that the changing chords bring to the lyric:

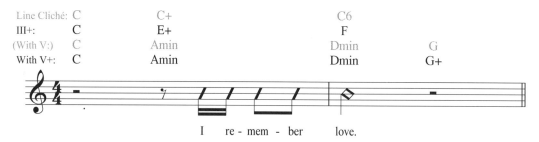

Line Cliché:	C	C+		C6	
III+:	C	E+		F	
(With V:)	C	Amin		Dmin	G
With V+:	C	Amin		Dmin	G+

I re - mem - ber love.

FIG. 21.11. Progression with Augmented Triads

This chart is a good visual guide to diatonic and borrowed chords most often found in popular music. Depending on the genre of music you are writing, you might find other chords to add to this chart that are not included.

Diatonic Triads:	C	Dmin	Emin	F	G	Amin	B°
Diatonic Sevenths:	CMaj7	Dmin7	Emin7	FMaj7	G7	Amin7	Bmin7♭5
Nondiatonic Triads:	Cmin	DMaj, D♭Maj	EMaj, E♭Maj	Fmin	Gmin	AMaj, A♭Maj	BMaj, B♭Maj
Nondiatonic Sevenths:		D♭Maj7	E♭Maj7	*Fmin7*	*Gmin7*	A♭Maj7	B♭Maj7
Minor 7♭5:		Dmin7♭5	Emin7♭5	F♯min7♭5	Gmin7♭5	Amin7♭5	
Diminished Triads:	C♯°	D♯°	E♭°	F♯°	G♯°		
Diminished Sevenths:	C♯°7	D♯°7	E♭°7	F♯°7	G♯°7		

FIG. 21.12. Diminished, Diminished Seventh, Minor 7♭5, and Augmented Chords

EXERCISES

Write a song section that uses an augmented chord in support of the emotion of the lyric, in the following ways:

1. In a line cliché: I I+ I6.

2. Moving from I to III+.

3. Ending a verse section with the V+ chord to set up the chorus.

22

Suspended, Add, and Power Chords

SUSPENDED CHORDS

Nothing makes storytelling better than adding suspense.

Sus4

The *sus4* chord is a triad. To find this chord, take a triad and substitute the 4 for the 3:

$$\text{Csus4} = \text{C, F, G} \qquad \text{Fsus4} = \text{F, B}\flat\text{, C} \qquad \text{Gsus4} = \text{G, C, D}$$

Sus4 chords add suspense and feel a bit hollow and open at the same time. This is because there is more distance between the 1 and the 4 than there is between the 1 and the 3.

Here are four ways you can use a sus4 chord:

1. First, you can use a sus4 chord as a substitute for the V chord at the end of a song section to introduce the next section. It's more dramatic than the regular V chord. Listen to this progression first with the regular V chord and then as a sus4 chord:

Audio 106

FIG. 22.1. V vs. Vsus4

The Vsus4 chord can be found in the following songs:

- "Skyfall" (Adele)
- "Just a Kiss" (Lady Antebellum)

Audio 107

2. Sus4 chords are often used in verses to build tension in support of the lyric.

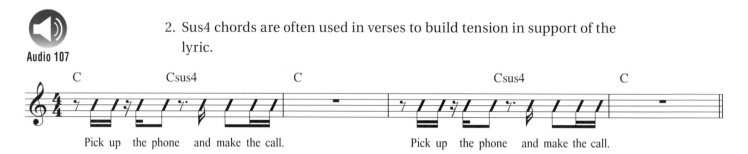

FIG. 22.2. Sus4 Supporting Lyric Tension

You can use the Isus4, IVsus4, or Vsus4 chord. Some examples:

* "It's So Hard to Say Goodbye to Yesterday" (Jason Mraz)
* "Shape of My Heart" (Backstreet Boys)

Audio 108

3. You can use the sus4 chord to add suspense to one particular word or words. Working again with the phrase:

I remember love

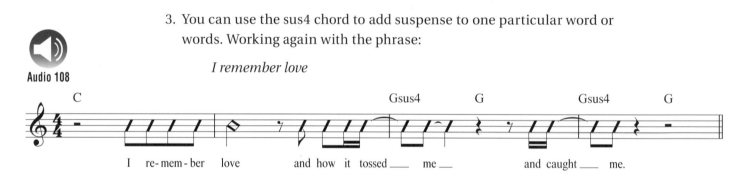

FIG. 22.3. Adding Suspense to a Word

Did you feel the tension placed on the words *tossed* and *caught*?

You can hear this at work in "Photograph" (Ed Sheeran).

Audio 109

4. In this example, the IVsus4 chord supports the feeling of suspension of being tossed and caught:

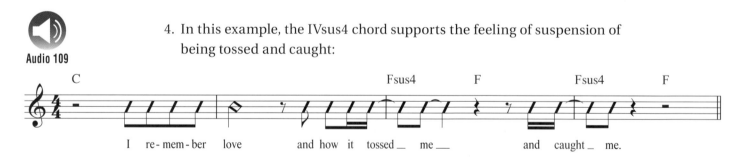

FIG. 22.4. Using IVsus4

An example is "Angel" (Sarah McLachlan).

Sus2

The other type of sus chord you can use is a sus2 chord. It can be used in the same ways as the sus4 chord. To find this chord, take a triad and substitute the 2 for the 3. Csus2 = C, D, G. This brings a more subtle form of tension. Let's see how it supports the lyric with the I chord:

Audio 110

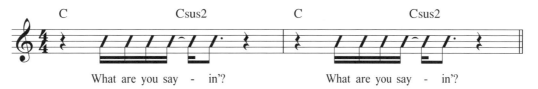

FIG. 22.5. Supporting a Lyric with Sus2

When the sus2 chord is used in the verses, it immediately sets up an atmosphere of suspense. Some examples of sus2 chords in the verse are:

- "Teenage Dream" (Katy Perry)
- "Call Me Maybe" (Carly Rae Jepsen)

Audio 111

The sus2 chord can also be used on the IV chord of a progression. Here is part of a chorus, using the IVsus2 chord following the VImin chord. Feel the tension:

FIG. 22.6. Using IVsus2

Do you feel how the sus2 chord supports the word *dreamed*?

- "Love Song" (Sara Bareilles) uses the IVsus2 chord in the verse to support how hard it is to breathe under water, and the overall angst of the song.

Sus4 in Minor

Audio 112

Let's look at the sus4 chord in the context of a minor key. Listen to the first four bars of the progression without the sus chord, and then notice the difference in sound and the effect in the next four bars when the sus4 chord substitutes for the regular major chord.

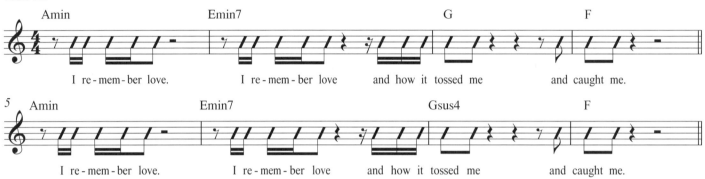

FIG. 22.7. Minor Key Sus4 Chord

Two examples:

- "Constant Craving" (k.d. lang) uses the VIIsus4 chord to color the lyric about the dark.
- "Somebody to Love'" (Jefferson Airplane)

EXERCISES

1. Write a verse using sus4 chords. Make sure you are using them in support of a lyric that is suspenseful or leading up to something suspenseful.

2. Rewrite the verse section using sus2 chords and note the difference that it brings to your song.

3. Write a song section where you pair one or two words with the sus4 or the sus2 chord.

ADD SOMETHING

Add2

Instead of suspending the 2, you can add it to the triad and call it a C(add2) chord: C D E G instead of C D G.

Audio 113

It still lends tension, but it's a warmer, subtler suspense that feels less open and empty. Listen again to the Csus2 chord, and then listen to it with the 3 also included.

FIG. 22.8. Csus2 (C D G) and C(add2) (C D E G)

C(add2) is a chord that contains the comfort of all three of the most stable notes in the key with an added note (the 2) to add some tension. This chord is used all the time in pop music.

Note: the symbols add2 and add9 are interchangeable. It is often spelled as add9.

Add4

The add4 (add11) works the same as the add2 chord except here, you are adding the 4: C E F G. This is adding the tension of the 4, but again, it's not as open and empty. It's a bit more stable than the sus4 because you have the major triad with the tension. This is another common chord in pop music.

Songs that contain the add4 chord:

- "Man in the Mirror" (Michael Jackson)
- "Fast Car" (Tracy Chapman)

EXERCISE

1. Write a song section using at least two add2 chords in support of the lyric.

2. Replace the add2 chords with sus2 chords and note the difference. Weigh how much tension or stability your lyric needs, and decide between the two.

3. Repeat the above steps using add4 instead of add2.

POWER CHORDS: LESS IS MORE

Sometimes, it's not *how many* notes you play, it's *which* notes you play. This is great news for non-instrumentalists or great singers who may feel intimidated playing an instrument.

Listen to the following example using the line:

This is me after you

- The first example is played with a C triad: C E G.
- The second example is played with just the power chord of an open fifth: the C and the G with no E:

Audio 114

FIG. 22.9. C Triad vs. C5 Power Chord

See? Less *is* more. Example 2 feels more sophisticated, and you're only playing two notes. Notice how open it sounds without the 3? As a ballad, it could support emptiness, or loneliness. It feels vulnerable and intimate. For an up-tempo rock song, it can feel powerful and strong. This chord is all over blues, rock, and popular music.

You will find the power chord in the following songs:

- "Fight Song" (Rachel Platten)
- "Put the Gun Down" (ZZ Ward)

EXERCISES

1. Write a verse to the following chord progression, with a lyric that reflects loneliness, vulnerability, isolation, etc. by omitting the 3 of every chord.

2. Write an up-tempo song section using only power chords or speed up one of your ballads. Notice how strong it feels.

FIG. 22.10. Practice Progression

23

Tensions: Mood Enhancers

Tensions are non-chord tones you can add to a chord to give it texture. Here is the C major scale, with its tensions.

FIG. 23.1. Tensions

Tensions are thought of as being built on top of a chord (i.e., extensions), therefore in a higher octave, but you can also play them down an octave. Tension 9 is the same as 2, 11 is the same as 4, and 13 is the same as 6. In music theory terms, they can be in any octave, but choosing a higher or lower octave will give a sense of added space or tension, respectively.

Chord Function	Tensions
IMaj7	9, 13
IImin7	9, 11, 13
IIImin7	11
IVMaj7	9, ♯11, 13
V7	9, 13
VImin7	9, 11
VIImin7♭5	11, ♭13

FIG. 23.2. Major Chord Functions
and Tensions

Think of tensions as literally adding tension to your chord and the lyric they are paired with. You could also think of them the way you do the notes in a major scale, as stable or unstable (refer back to lesson 8 on tonal gravity).

Listen to the following example and how the shifting tensions affect the narrative:

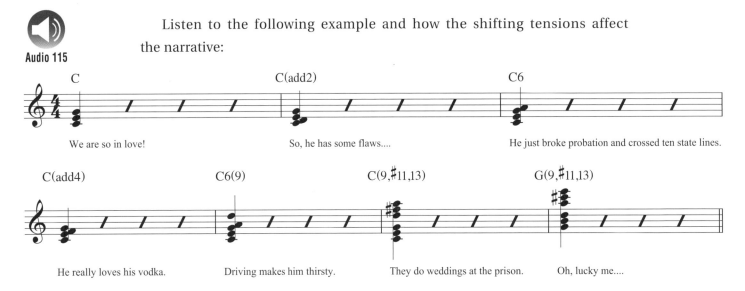

FIG. 23.3. A Tension Narrative

- C: The story begins on the major triad.

- C(add2): The 2 adds the least amount of tension because it's so close to the home note, and it's supported by the stable triad. It adds just enough angst to let you know that something isn't perfect.

- C6: Adding the 6 up high supports the tension of this guy on the move.

- C(add4): This is a more stable dissonance than a sus4 chord, but the added 4 really lets that dissonance color his drinking.

- C6(9): Comparatively, this is not as tense sounding, but it's tense and it's bringing back the distance with those two notes being so far away from the home note, supporting the stress of drinking and driving.

- C(9,♯11,13): What's more tense than a wedding at a prison? All tensions on board for that line.

- G(9,♯11,13): The V chord also needs the deluxe package of tensions because it supports the delusional bride.

You can start by altering a chord in a progression by adding a non-chord tone to see what it brings to the chord. A tension a half step away will add more tension than will a tension that is a whole step from a chord tone.

EXERCISES

1. Write a melody and lyric to the following chord progression in response to the emotions of the chords. Articulate why you paired each lyric with its respective chord.

FIG. 23.4. Tension Practice

2. Write a verse and a chorus with your own chord progression, using at least two tensions in support of the content of your lyric.

24

Writing in a Minor Key

Writing in a minor key is usually associated with sadness. But it also brings the darkness, the sinister, the creepy, the angry, and, depending on the groove, the sexy.

NATURAL MINOR

Most popular songs that are written in minor are written in natural minor. Here are the available diatonic chords in the key of A minor:

Diatonic Triads:	Imin	II°	♭III	IVmin	Vmin	♭VI	♭VII

FIG. 24.1. Available Diatonic Chords in Natural Minor

Like the major key, the minor key can also borrow chords from outside the key. There are not as many borrowed chords because you are usually writing in a minor key for the specific musical flavor it brings to your song.

When you get tired of the available diatonic chords in natural minor, try adding the leading tone (raised 7) in the melody, or borrowing chords (usually ♭IIMaj or VMaj). The VMaj gives your song a stronger cadence than the diatonic Vmin due to the leading tone.

In the following chart, the first line shows the available diatonic triads for a minor key. Then, the most common chords you can use to expand your harmonic palette:

Diatonic Triads:	Imin	II°	♭III	IVmin	Vmin	♭VI	♭VII
In C Minor:	Cmin	D°	E♭Maj	Fmin	Gmin	A♭	B♭
Sevenths:	Cmin7	Dmin7♭5	E♭Maj7	Fmin7	Gmin7	A♭Maj7	B♭7
Commonly Borrowed:		♭IIMaj D♭Maj			VMaj GMaj	VImin7♭5 Amin7♭5	
Dominant Sevenths:				IV7 F7	V7 G7		

FIG. 24.2. Expanded Minor Key Palette

ADDING TENSIONS IN MINOR

These tensions are commonly used in minor keys:

Chord Function	Tensions
Imin7	9, 11, 13
II°7	11, ♭13
♭IIIMaj7	9, 13
IVmin7	9, 11, 13
Vmin7	11
♭VIMaj7	9, ♯11, 13
♭VII7	9, 13

FIG. 24.3. Minor Chord Functions
and Tensions

The most important thing to focus on when deciding on a chord progression in minor is what the chords will bring to your song and offer your lyrics, tempo and groove. Experiment with different chords to see what emotional nuance they are bringing. Here are some chord progressions you can try in the minor key:

Imin IVmin ♭VI ♭VII	"Shape of You" (Ed Sheeran)
Imin ♭III ♭VII ♭VI	"Hello" (Adele)
Imin ♭VII IV	"Hurricane" (*Hamilton*)
Imin ♭VII	"Somebody That I Used to Know" (Gotye)
Imin Vmin Imin Vmin	"Fallin'" (Alicia Keys)
Imin ♭VI ♭III ♭VII	"Broken-Hearted Girl" (Beyoncé)
Imin ♭VII ♭VI	"I'll Show You" (Justin Bieber)
Imin IVmin	"Take Me to Church" (Hozier)

FIG. 24.4. Chord Progressions in Minor Key

25

Modes

So far, we've delved deeply into the major key and what it has to offer your writing. We've looked at natural minor and its inherent brand of darkness. But here in this chapter, we will look at writing in a mode. There are several modes to choose from, but in this chapter, we will look at the two most popular modes used in pop music: Mixolydian and Dorian.

MIXOLYDIAN

Mixolydian is very closely related to the major key. To find Mixolydian, play the major scale. Change one note, and you have Mixolydian:

Audio 116

FIG. 25.1. G Mixolydian

It's important to know this mode's signature melody note is the ♭7, and to use it to emphasize the mode so that it doesn't sound like a major key.

Here are the available chords in Mixolydian:

Triads:	I	IImin	III°	IV	Vmin	VImin	♭VII
Sevenths:	I7	IImin7	IIImin7♭5	IVMaj7	Vmin7	VImin7	♭VIIMaj7

FIG. 25.2. Diatonic Triads and Seventh Chords of Mixolydian

You can bring out the Mixolydian mood using the I chord and letting the melody do the work of highlighting the ♭7, or use a Mixolydian chord progression to capture the character of this mode.

Here are some typical chord progressions you can try in Mixolydian, paired with some songs that use them.

I ♭VII, I ♭VII IV	"Royals" (Lorde)
I ♭VII IV	"White Liar" (Miranda Lambert)
I ♭VII	"Seven Bridges Road" (Eagles)

EXERCISES

1. Write a verse section using only the I chord of the Mixolydian scale, emphasizing the mode melodically.

2. Write a verse and chorus section with one of the following chord progressions to emphasize the Mixolydian mode:

    *   I ♭VII
    *   I ♭VII IV

DORIAN

Dorian brings another interesting mood to the table, and its effect can vary (like all keys and modes) depending on the tempo and groove you use.

Dorian is a great choice for dance tunes because it doesn't have a strong cadence like a major key does. In a slower ballad, it can bring a unique minor feel to your song.

To find a Dorian melody, start in a major key on the second note of the scale and go up from there. This will give you the Dorian mode. It is beyond the scope of this book to go deeply into the theory of this mode, but you can borrow and mix and match from the composite of the four minor scales: natural minor, harmonic minor, Dorian, and melodic minor.

Here is D Dorian. The signature note is the sixth scale degree.

Audio 117

FIG. 25.3. D Dorian

Here are the available chords in Dorian:

Diatonic Triads:	Imin	IImin	♭III	IV	Vmin	VI°	♭VII
Seventh Chords:	Imin7	IImin7	♭IIIMaj7	IV7	Vmin7	VImin7♭5	♭VIIMaj7

FIG. 25.4. Diatonic Triads and Seventh Chords of Dorian

Here is a list of songs in Dorian and the chords they use:

Imin IV	"It's Too Late" (Carole King). Verse.
Imin7 IV/I	"Be Still My Beating Heart" (Sting)
Imin IV/I	"You Oughta Know" (Alanis Morissette)
Imin ♭VII	"Stayin' Alive" (Bee Gees)
Imin IVMaj7 VIMaj7 IV7	"Drive" (Incubus)
Imin ♭IIIMaj ♭VII IV	"What Goes Around Comes Around" (Justin Timberlake)
Imin7 ♭III Vmin7 IV	"Get Lucky" (Daft Punk)

FIG. 25.5. Dorian Progressions

EXERCISES

1. Write a song section on only the Imin chord. Bring out the flavor of the Dorian mode in your melody, placing special attention to highlighting the character note: 6.

2. Write an up-tempo song section using the following chord progression: Imin ♭III Vmin IV.

3. Write a song section using the chords: Imin IV.

26

Harmonic Rhythm in 4/4

It's hard to make *harmonic rhythm* sound sexy, but like with the nerdy guy in high school who everyone ignored, who became a tech tycoon, they all wished they had taken the time to get to know him better.

Harmonic rhythm determines how many beats a chord will last before you change to the next chord.

Let's say you have a verse section with a harmonic rhythm of two chords per measure, where each chord is played for two beats. Your harmonic rhythm is then two chords per measure with two beats each. You could change the harmonic rhythm in the chorus to create contrast by using a slower harmonic rhythm, playing each chord for four beats.

Audio 118

FIG. 26.1. Slower Harmonic Rhythm in the Chorus

Did you feel the chorus slow down?

Or you could write a prechorus with a faster harmonic rhythm, accelerating and helping the prechorus move into the chorus. Play the following example. Feel the motion of the harmony speed up in the prechorus and then slow down for the chorus.

Audio 119

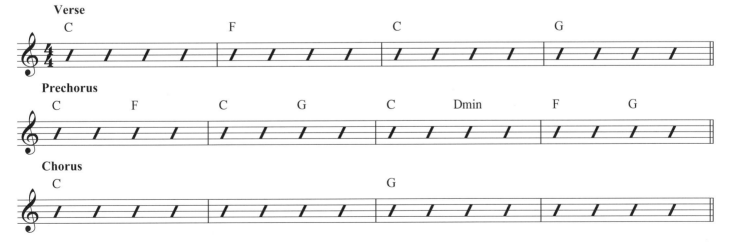

FIG. 26.2. Faster Harmonic Rhythm in the Prechorus

Did you feel the contrast between the different sections?

CHOOSING HARMONIC RHYTHM

Some writers start with an established chord progression that they borrow from another song, inheriting a pre-existing harmonic rhythm.

Changing your harmonic rhythm between song sections is a great tool for creating contrast, but it can also be used to support the meaning of your lyrics and help you tell your story.

Take a look at the following lyric setting of the song "Apogee. In this song, the singer is emotionally bound to someone who isn't safe to love.

The chords are changing so quickly, it's distracting and the harmonic rhythm isn't serving the story. This is where using harmonic rhythm gets interesting. So let's give this nerd a chance and see what happens!

Audio 120

FIG. 26.3. "Apogee" Verse with Two Chords per Measure

By slowing down the harmonic rhythm, you slow down your listener along with it. The melody is helping to create the push and pull and emotional angst by using the unstable 6 throughout, and the chords play their part, but our focus for this chapter is on the harmonic rhythm. By intentionally choosing a slower harmonic rhythm that supports lyrics like: *Hold me in place, heaviest grace,* and *gravity,* you come closer to offering the listener the *experience the singer is having.* Now, let's slow the harmonic rhythm down to one chord per measure.

Audio 121

FIG. 26.4. "Apogee" with One Chord Per Measure

How did that feel? The content and harmonic rhythm are in closer alignment, but we are trying to support the idea of being emotionally bound to someone. So let's slow the harmonic rhythm down even further to create a bit more weight, and add a prechorus:

Audio 122

FIG. 26.5. "Apogee" with Slower Harmonic Rhythm

How does it feel now? Did you slow down along with the harmonic motion? Although the melody is moving, the harmony anchors you. The harmonic rhythm is supporting the singer wanting to be free (the melody) but held in place by the power the other person has over them (the harmonic rhythm). Did you feel how well the ♭III chord influences the word *suspended*? When you match *what* you're saying with *how* you are saying it, you take your listener from observer to participant, giving them a deeper experience of your song.

EXERCISES

1. Write a verse using harmonic rhythm to support the emotion of your lyric. Find a metaphor that calls for a slow harmonic rhythm. You could use a word like *anchor* or something concrete like a small hometown. Aim your content towards being held down by something, be it a town, a relationship, a belief, a fear, etc. Use one or two chords per measure.

2. Write a chorus with a faster harmonic rhythm that supports the opposite of being held down. Maybe now, you're leaving that town, forgiving the past, releasing the fear, etc.

3. Write a new verse and chorus, giving your verse a fast harmonic rhythm of at least two chords per measure, slowing your chorus down to one chord per measure in support of your lyric.

HIGHLIGHTING WITH HARMONIC RHYTHM

So far, we've looked at the effect of contrasting harmonic rhythm between song sections, but you can also use this tool for a single measure to highlight an important lyrical moment.

When you play a consistent harmonic rhythm for several measures, and then change the harmonic rhythm by holding a chord longer than expected, you anchor your listener in place for that moment. When you break the flow of the expected meter, it highlights your lyric.

Listen to the harmonic pattern in the following example:

Audio 123

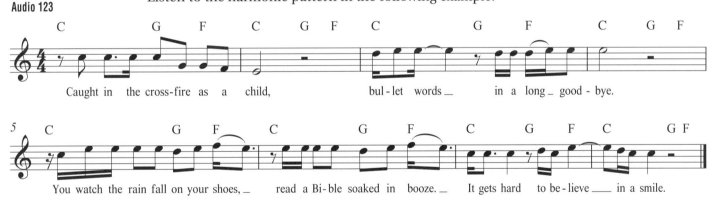

FIG. 26.6. "Crossfire" Harmonic Pattern

The harmonic rhythm is consistent for eight measures, so the only musical elements working to make the lyrics stand out are the changes of the melody and melodic rhythm in measures 5 and 6 and the rhyme scheme of *shoes/booze*.

The metaphor of *bullet words* is powerful, but the line that holds the most story is:

> *Read a Bible soaked in booze.*

Booze is a loaded word in this verse. The juxtaposition of *a Bible soaked in booze* covers a lot of ground in just a few words. Is one of the parents an alcoholic? Are they religious? Are they hypocrites? Is the dad an alcoholic minister? That's a line worth highlighting.

Audio 124

Let's put the focus on that lyric by changing the harmonic rhythm in measure 7, drawing out the F chord for an unexpected three additional beats.

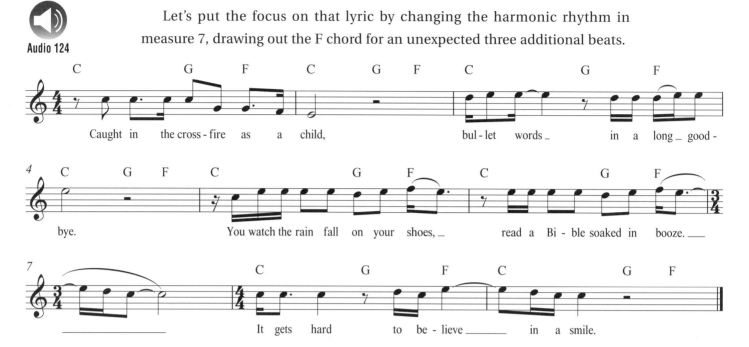

FIG. 26.7. "Crossfire" with Extended F Chord in Measure 7

The unexpected harmonic rhythm held you in place by the extra, unexpected three beats. When you hold a chord unexpectedly to accent a lyric, it's called an *agogic accent*.

EXERCISE

1. Write an eight-bar song section with two or three chords per measure.

2. Break your harmonic pattern by lengthening the harmonic rhythm unexpectedly after at least six bars to highlight an essential lyric.

27

Harmonic Rhythm in 3/4

So far, you've looked at how harmonic rhythm can create contrast, control motion, and highlight a lyric. Changing up your time signature can bring something fresh to your songs. Let's look at harmonic rhythm in 3/4.

Typically, songs in 3/4 use the harmonic rhythm of one chord per measure, where the chord is played on the first beat of each measure.

Audio 125

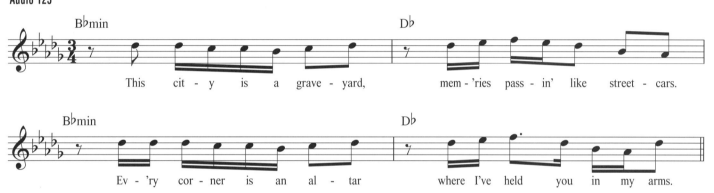

FIG. 27.1. One Chord Per Measure

Audio 126

This is interesting due to the meter, but let's add a chord to each measure to add even more interest:

FIG. 27.2. Adding Chords on Beat 2

The harmonic rhythm is unexpected and interesting simply because the harmony is changing in a unique place in the bar: beat two. When you change the chord unexpectedly, your listener pays closer attention to the lyric on that change.

What story do the highlighted words tell?

city, passin', corner, held

It's not a bad list, but what about these words?

graveyard, streetcars, altar, arms

These words leave a deeper imprint. As a list, they are more specific and bring more associations.

Let's see if we can have the best of both worlds by having a unique harmonic rhythm *and* highlighting the most important lyrics, by moving the chords from beat 2 to beat 3. We'll add an extra four bars of lyric to reveal a bit more of the story. Take a listen:

Audio 127

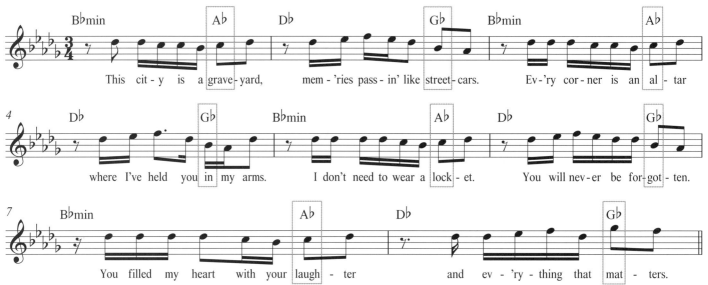

FIG. 27.3. Chords on Beats 1 and 3

With the shift of the chord placement, we've highlighted the words that hold the most meaning. Now, let's turn up the emotion and let you know how the singer *feels*. Let's add an unexpected measure, changing the time signature to 4/4 to highlight the lyric in measure 9, before it goes into the chorus:

I miss you, I wish you'd

In the following example, measure 9 highlights the lyric using an agogic accent:

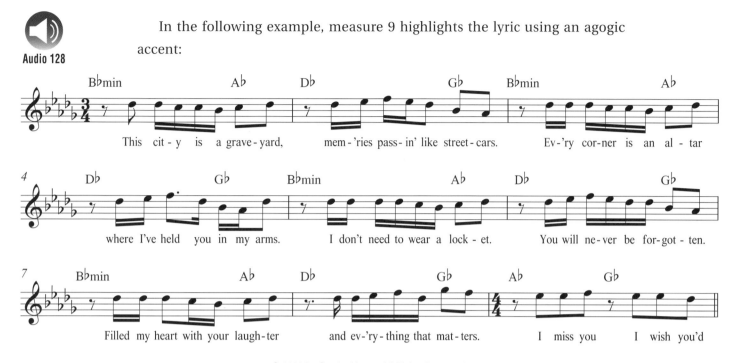

FIG. 27.4. Agogic Accent in Bar 9

How did that feel? The last line of a section always gets special emphasis because it's the last thing being said, but it's highlighted even more here due to the changes in harmonic rhythm, the change in meter, and an unexpected measure.

EXERCISES

1. Write a verse section in 3/4 or 6/8.

2. Find a unique harmonic rhythm.

3. Change the harmonic rhythm to highlight the most important words in the lyric.

4. Add an additional line to the lyric. Make sure the line is something you want to highlight and change the meter in the extra measure to a bar of 4/4.

28

Direct Modulation

Modulation occurs when you leave your current key and establish a new key in another location within your song. A key change adds interest, contrast, and emotional intensity, and *it can support the meaning of your lyric.* Here are two ways to modulate:

1. Direct Modulation

2. Pivot Modulation

You can modulate as high or as low as you or your singer will feel comfortable singing. Here are some of the common ways that songs modulate, and some of the locations where modulations take place:

Typical Destinations of Modulations	Locations of Modulations
• Half step up or down: C to D♭ or C to B • Whole step up or down: C to D or C to B♭ • Relative major to relative minor: C major to A minor • Relative minor to relative major: A minor to C major • Parallel minor to parallel major: C minor to C major • Parallel major to parallel minor: C major to C minor • Subdominant modulation: major key up a fourth to its subdominant region • Dominant modulation: major key up a fifth or down a fourth to its dominant region	• Intro to verse • Verse to prechorus • Prechorus to chorus • Chorus to verse • Chorus to bridge • Post-chorus • Chorus to chorus to chorus

FIG. 28.1. Typical Modulation Behavior in Popular Songs

A *direct modulation* is abrupt. You go right into a new key without any musical hint of the new destination key. Most people associate direct modulation with the diva on the stage modulating each chorus until glass starts to shatter.

"Love on Top" (Beyoncé) modulates four times in the later choruses, up a half step every time. It supports the lyric as the key modulates up on the title, "Love on Top."

In the following song, there's a direct modulation from the chorus into the second verse. Listen to the modulation, up a whole step from the key of C to the key of D. There is no harmonic introduction—just a quick melody foreshadowing the upcoming key.

Audio 129

FIG. 28.2. Direct Modulation from Chorus into Verse

The modulation creates interest where there has been a repetitive chord progression for the verse and the chorus. It modulates on the words *Shrug off that mean voice,* drawing attention to one of the most important lyrics in the song. The modulation going up supports being more positive.

You may decide that this is too abrupt or possibly difficult to sing each time because you don't have a harmonic hint of the next key. This is where the second type of modulation (pivot) comes in.

29

Pivot-Chord Modulation

If you are in the key of C and want to modulate to the key of D, for a smoother transition, you can introduce the new key with a pivot chord, shared by both keys.

To create a pivot-chord modulation, find a chord that is common to both the current key *and* the destination key.

To find a common chord, list the chords in both keys, and find the chords they share:

C Major	I	IImin	IIImin	IV	V	VImin	VII°	V of C
	C	Dmin	Emin	F	G	Amin	B°	
D Major	I	IImin	IIImin	IV	V	VImin	VII°	IV of D
	D	Emin	F♯min	G	A	Bmin	C♯°	

FIG. 29.1. Finding the Common Chord

The shared chord has to have the same chord quality. If you look at the list from the keys of C and D, they have two chords in common: G major and E minor. We will use G major in our example.

You can hear how the G chord sets your ear up for the new key. In figure 29.2, notice that the measure before the chorus now has the common G chord with a common note A in the bass, to create the hybrid chord G/A. The last three notes before the modulation also introduce the new key. Both keys share D7(9). The first two notes, D and E, belong to the new key. F♯ belongs to the new key.

Audio 130

FIG. 29.2. Pivot Chord G/A in Bar 9

It's common to use the V chord of the destination key to set up the modulation as well, but it's not as smooth as the subtler move of the G/A. The V chord of D major, the destination key, is A major. The A major chord isn't diatonic to the home key of C major, but the A *minor* chord is, and it shares two common chord tones with A major:

- A minor: A C E
- A major: A C♯ E

Audio 131

The V chord of the destination key is a clean, quick introduction to the new key:

FIG. 29.3. Adding A, the V of D

THE INTRO

The chorus isn't the only place in your song where you can modulate: the intro is another interesting possibility. You could modulate from a major-key intro into another major key in the verse, or you could try modulating from a minor key directly to its parallel major key.

The choice of the minor intro adds a musical surprise right away when it changes unexpectedly in the verse. It can support the meaning of the lyric by foreshadowing what's to come later on in the song when the chorus lyric turns dark:

Audio 132

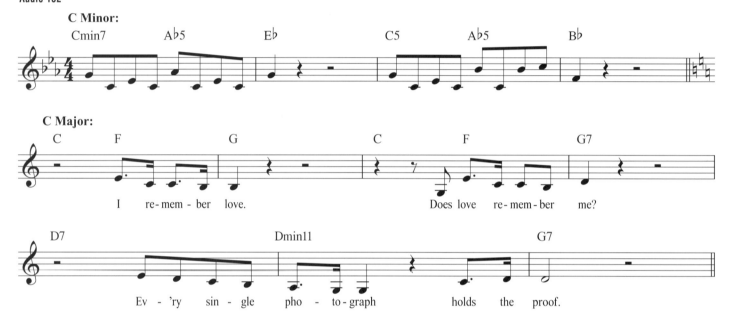

FIG. 29.4. Modulation from Intro into Verse. Intro is in C minor, verse is in C Major.

Songs that use minor-to-major modulations:

- "You've Got a Friend" (Carole King). The intro is in A♭ major, setting up contrast for the dark feeling of the verse in F minor. The chorus modulates to relative A♭ major, using the pivot chord C minor, which is common between both F minor and A♭ major.

- "One" (U2) uses the relative-minor-to-major modulation. The verse is in A minor, and the chorus goes to C major.

THE BRIDGE

Writers are always looking for new ways to approach writing the bridge to their song. Modulating in the bridge is a way to create something really unique and unexpected.

Let's work again with "Apogee." The song is in the key of A major. The destination key in this case is the key of C. To set the ear up for the modulation, we'll use common notes in both keys: B and A.

- In A major, the notes B and A are the 2 and 1.
- In C major, the notes B and A are the 7 and 6.

Audio 133

Listen to the chorus leading into the modulating bridge and then back out again to the home key, using a pivot melody to get back to A major. Notice the pivot melody on the pickup line to the chorus: *When I'm* (in bar 32).

FIG. 29.5. Pivot Melody Modulation in Bar 32

This modulation is surprising and interesting, and it supports the meaning of the lyric. The song modulates down from A to C, supporting the hopelessness of *I'm gonna keep on lovin' you* (measures 23 and 27). Then, the line *I wait for the light* (measure 31) has the longest note of the phrase being held on the word *light*. The bridge is waiting for the light of the next modulated chorus which modulates back up to the key of A, bringing *light*. In measure 25, the F chord feels like the ♭VI chord in the home key of A major, but it's also the IV chord in the new key of C major. It's the common chord shared by both keys. It's sharing melody and harmony.

An example of a chorus that modulates into a bridge is "Heartbreak Warfare" (John Mayer). In his modulation, it goes from the key of A major down to F major using a pivot melody. The bridge modulation supports the lyrical content where he talks about being high and then how far she can make him fall. It's perfect prosody, because it modulates down.

EXERCISES

Pick three of the following modulations, and try them with your original songs:

1. Write a minor key intro that moves into a major key verse section.
   Use prosody, letting the minor intro foreshadow something emotional,
   sad, or dark to come later in a chorus section.

2. Rewrite your intro in a major key that moves into a minor verse.
   Use prosody in the minor verse to support your lyric.

3. Write a chorus that modulates into the second verse.
   Use direct modulation.

4. Write the same chorus modulating into the verse using a pivot chord
   modulation.

5. Write a bridge that modulates into another key using a pivot melody.

6. Write a verse in minor and a chorus in its parallel major.

7. Write a verse in minor that modulates to its relative major in the chorus.

PART III
Form: Unforgettable and Signature Song Sections

Up to this point, you've gone deeply into the craft of harmony and melody. Now, it's time to transfer those skills to the actual part you play beneath your amazing songs and how you introduce them musically to your listener from the very first note. A well-crafted intro and signature part written for each song section can make a good song great. What would "Jump" by Van Halen be without that unique synth intro or "Walking in Memphis" by Marc Cohn be without the arpeggio piano part?

Using the skills you've gained so far, we'll look at unforgettable intros and signature song sections. Then, we'll look at standard song form and learn about new forms and current song sections that make up todays commercial hits, with exercises to create your own unique sections and overall form. As with every technique in this book, the part you write and the form you choose can also be used to help you tell your story.

Intros

The crowd is waiting for the concert to start. The band plays the first couple of notes and the fans start screaming. That first bar is like the fuse of dynamite being lit. That's because in addition to writing a hit song, the band wrote a signature intro as well. An intro so memorable, you know it from the first few notes.

It's not enough to strum or play through your chord progression and call it an intro. When you take your time to craft something special and memorable, you make a good song even better and grab your listeners' attention right away. Music supervisors, artists, and management hear several songs a day and they are busy—so hook them from the first note!

Your intro can be its own unique composition or something that you thread throughout the song.

Here are several ways to approach writing an intro:

1. Melodic intro. This can be an original melody, a melody from your chorus, or a melody from another song section, used as foreshadowing.
   - "Stairway to Heaven" (Led Zeppelin)
   - "See You Again" (Wiz Khalifa feat. Charlie Puth)
   - "100 Years" (Five for Fighting)
2. Arpeggiation. This is an arpeggiated part usually played on piano or guitar.
   - "Attention" (Charlie Puth)
   - "Grenade" (Bruno Mars)
   - "Clocks" (Coldplay)
3. Bass line. This is a unique rhythm and melody played on the bass.
   - "Come Together" (the Beatles)
   - "My Girl" (the Temptations)
   - "Give Me One Reason" (Tracy Chapman)
4. Synth sound. This is an intro using an electronic instrument.
   - "Silence" (Marshmello feat. Khalid)
   - "Jump" (Van Halen)
   - "Slide" (Calvin Harris)

5. Distinctive sound.

- "Come Together" (the Beatles), the "shhh" part
- "Boyfriend" (Justin Bieber)
- "Moves Like Jagger" (Maroon 5), the guitar groove and whistled hook

6. Signature drum part. The style of the drum part can support the lyric. A military-influenced beat could support bravery, or a more simple drum beat could set up the emotion and serve as the singer's heartbeat, or it could simply be a really unique groove.

- "50 Ways to Leave Your Lover" (Paul Simon)
- "Brave" (Sara Bareilles)
- "My Sharona" (the Knack)

7. Riff or groove.

- "Layla" (Eric Clapton)
- "Back in Black" (AC/DC)
- "Start Me Up" (the Rolling Stones)

8. Unique melodic and rhythmic pattern.

- "A Thousand Miles" (Vanessa Carlton)
- "100 Years" (Five for Fighting)

9. A cappella.

- "Take a Chance on Me" (ABBA)
- "Seven Bridges Road" (the Eagles)
- "Army" (Ben Folds Five)

10. Unexpected harmonic rhythm in 4/4 or 3/4.

- "Love Song" (Sara Bareilles)
- "Closer" (the Chainsmokers)
- "Take Me to Church" (Hozier)

11. Ostinato bass or other part.

- "Too High" (Stevie Wonder)
- "Attention" (Charlie Puth)
- "All My Friends" (LCD Soundsystem)

12. Musical drone.

- "Hanging by a Moment" (Lifehouse)
- "Teenage Dream" (Katy Perry)
- "I Still Haven't Found What I'm Looking For" (U2)

Writing interesting parts doesn't have to stop at your intro. Take these ideas into each section of your song. If your intro and verse have arpeggios, you might decide to bring in a fresh rhythmic part on guitar for your chorus. Or maybe you want to use an ostinato bass part in your intro and verse and write an arpeggio for your chorus. Think about how you can make each section grow and change throughout your song to keep it interesting.

EXERCISES

1. Choose one of the following chord progressions or one of your own, and write three different types of intros.

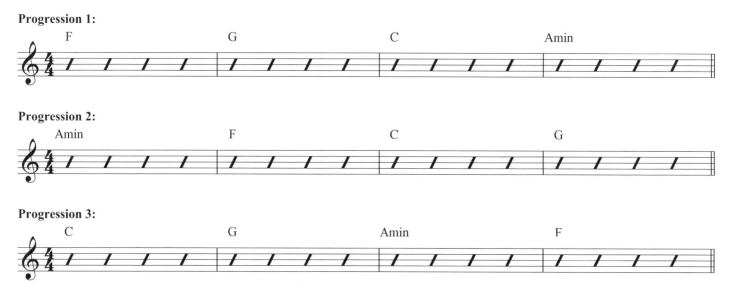

FIG. 30.1. Practice Progressions

2. Write an original intro for one of your original songs.

3. Write a new accompanying part for your chorus or bridge, and write an outro.

Basic Song Forms

When you write a new song, choosing a common form helps your listener navigate through your story and organizes your ideas into different sections. The standard verse/chorus song allows the listener to expect to hear the details of the story in the verses and to anticipate the main idea with repetition in the upcoming chorus so they can sing along.

Once you are comfortable with the typical forms, you might decide to begin your song with the chorus, or write a new unidentifiable section that will surprise your listener and make your song more unique and familiar.

We will explore the building blocks of popular song structure:

- Verse
- Prechorus
- Chorus
- Post-chorus
- Bridge
- Drop
- Outro

AAA

The AAA song form consists of verse sections that begin or end with a *refrain* line. The refrain is typically one line and it is usually the title of the song, set to its own distinctive melody, rhythm, and harmony. The content of the lyric should be written to the refrain line like a joke written to its punch line. All content should point to the title of the song. Here's a lyric co-written with Mark Shilansky.

Refrain at the end:

> *When there's no proof that love was ever here*
>
> *And I can't recall why I cried that last tear*
>
> *Somehow out of nowhere the memory of your laughter reappears*
>
> *Like an old forgotten song*
>
> **[Refrain]** *Every good-bye ain't gone*

Refrain at the beginning:

> **[Refrain]** *Every good-bye ain't gone*
>
> *The heart holds one*
>
> *So I let myself remember though I swore I'd know better*
>
> *The smile I'd long forgotten like an old folded letter*
>
> *The mention of your name feels like rain then a downpour I can't stop*

Typically, the melody and harmony stay the same in each verse. Since the music doesn't change, the listener can focus on your lyric without the distraction of a changing musical backdrop. Due to the repetition of the music, it's important that the verse lyric develop the story and deepen in content with each new verse section.

ᴀAA

When the verse ends with a refrain, ending the section on the tonic note and tonic chord will make it feel complete. This closes the section, like ending a sentence with a period.

Verse/Refrain	Verse/Refrain	Verse/Refrain
Or		
Refrain/Verse	Refrain/Verse	Refrain/Verse

Some AAA songs:

- "Cold, Cold Heart" (Hank Williams). The refrain appears at the end of each A section.

- "The First Time Ever I Saw Your Face" (Roberta Flack). Each verse begins with the refrain lyric, *The first time ever I saw your face.* The story grows as the content of each verse changes.

- Maverick move: "You're Gonna Live Forever in Me" (John Mayer) is an AAA song form with an additional line following the refrain. The refrain title closes down with the tonic, and then there is a surprise line that is musically open, where he says, *I guarantee.* The added surprise line really gets attention because it's unexpected and is a great way to highlight an important lyric.

AABA

In an AABA song, the A sections are typically musically identical, and the B section (bridge) has new music that contrasts with A. The AABA song form is therefore an extension of the AAA song. In its standard form, it's known to be 32 bars long with each section containing 8 bars.

The *bridge* in a verse/refrain song is different from the bridge of a verse/chorus song. The B section of a verse/refrain typically follows the first two verse sections and is typically eight bars long. The bridge differs musically from a chorus in that it feels like more of a place you are visiting rather than a place you call home. The A section feels like home.

The function of the B section is to create musical and lyrical contrast. It might make an emotional statement that ties all the A sections together or offers a philosophical viewpoint. Either way, the bridge takes you someplace new, so make sure you are saying something different and worthy of the attention a new song section receives.

Verse/Refrain	Verse/Refrain	Bridge	Verse/Refrain

As with the AAA form, each verse can begin or end with the refrain line.

The first two examples below end with the refrain. Both have eight-measure verses with the refrain placed as the last line. The first three lines rhyme, but the title does not rhyme, making the title/refrain stand out even more.

- "Make You Feel My Love" (Bob Dylan)
- "Into the Mystic" (Van Morrison)

The next two examples begin with the refrain:

- "Come Away with Me" (Norah Jones)
- "Yesterday" (the Beatles)

ABAB

The chorus is the section of the song where your audience gets to sing along with you. The chorus shouldn't sound like any other song section, so contrast is crucial. The music and lyric typically repeat exactly the same each time the chorus is sung. Occasionally, the lyric will change depending on the needs of your story. You will often find the highest note of the song sung in the chorus, along with the main point and the title, with repetition.

Your song can have either one or two verses, before the chorus, depending on how much information is needed to set up each chorus.

Verse	Chorus	Verse	Chorus

The title can be placed:

- At the beginning of the chorus.
- At the end of the chorus.
- At the beginning and end of the chorus.
- Repeated throughout the chorus.

ABAB songs include:

- "It's Too Late" (Carole King). Title occurs at the beginning of the chorus.
- "Mama's Broken Heart" (Miranda Lambert). Title occurs at the end of the chorus.
- "I Can't Make You Love Me" (Bonnie Raitt)
- "I Will Always Love You" (Whitney Houston)

ABABCB: ADDING A BRIDGE

In a chorus song, a bridge should add something new, either by making a philosophical point, saying something that gives new meaning to the chorus that follows it, or advancing the story. The bridge should sound different from any of the other song sections and typically lasts four to eight bars.

Verse	Chorus	Verse	Chorus	Bridge	Chorus

Some ABABCB songs:

- "100 Years" (Five for Fighting). The bridge in this song does some heavy lifting, lyrically advancing the story as it ages the singer from age 45 to 67.
- "Walking in Memphis" (Marc Cohn). This bridge takes the song somewhere deeper, emotionally.
- Maverick move: "All About That Bass" (Meghan Trainor) begins the song with the chorus.

ABCABCDC: ADDING A PRECHORUS

The *prechorus* comes before the chorus and should feel like it's in motion, taking you somewhere. It's often referred to as "the climb," as many prechoruses ascend melodically, pulling you up to the chorus.

Verse	Prechorus	Chorus	Verse	Prechorus	Chorus	Bridge	Chorus

The prechorus should feel like its own distinctive piece of music. If you were to play it separately from the rest of the song, it should feel like its own unique composition. It ranges from two to eight bars in length:

- "Love Song" (Sara Bareilles) is eight bars.

- "Firework" (Katy Perry) is eight bars.

- "Love Yourself" (Justin Bieber) has two prechorus sections before his chorus: AB^1B^2C.

Verse	PC 1	PC 2	Chorus

THROUGH-COMPOSED

A through-composed song has different music for each song section with no repeated sections.

- "You'll Never Walk Alone" (Josh Groban). The through-composed music for this lyric is perfect prosody. It supports the story of going through unexpected things in life, never knowing what will happen next, one difficulty after another, but never having to walk alone.

32

Hybrid Song Forms

Song forms evolve, and once you understand standard song form, you might want to change it by combining elements of form or creating a new section.

Let's look at a hybrid of the traditional AABA song form:

AABaA

Here, the B section is also tagged with the refrain line:

Verse/Refrain	Verse/Refrain	Bridge/Refrain	Verse/Refrain

Songs that tag the B section with the refrain:

- "Humble and Kind" (Tim McGraw)
- "What We Ain't Got" (Jake Owen)

OUTRO

An outro is a unique and separate section that brings your song to a close. It can be added to the end of a verse/refrain song or a chorus song.

- "What Sarah Said" (Death Cab for Cutie)
- "Hey Jude" (the Beatles). The outro at the end of this song feels like an epic chorus where everyone sings the non-lexical vocals: *Nah nah nah...* with the title interspersed as everyone sings together.
- "Oh, Pretty Woman" (Roy Orbison) breaks form with two completely different bridge sections: AAB^1B^2AC.

Verse	Verse	Bridge 1	Bridge 2	Verse	Outro

33

New Song Sections: Post-Chorus, Drop, and Tag

POST-CHORUS

A newer song section in popular music today is the *post-chorus*. Just when you think you have heard the chorus, there's another section that is just as interesting, and might feel as big or bigger than the official chorus.

- "Chandelier" (Sia). The chorus is sixteen bars long, and the post-chorus is eight bars long. The post-chorus has a new melody and a new lyric but the same chord progression as the chorus. The chorus contains the title.

Verse	Prechorus	Chorus	Post-chorus

- "Shape of You" (Ed Sheeran) has a post-chorus section, with a hook on the words *oh I* interspersed with the hook line.

Verse	Prechorus	Chorus	Post-chorus

- "Can't Stop the Feeling!" by Justin Timberlake is a complex song form.

Verse	Prechorus 1	Prechorus 2	Chorus	Post-chorus

The idea of the title line, "Can't Stop the Feeling," is supported by the fact that five times in a row, you get a new song section and each section feels bigger emotionally until you finally get to the post-chorus. You can't stop the new song sections or the feelings! Great prosody with this song form.

DROP

The *drop* section has been used for years by DJs and in EDM music and is currently showing up all over pop radio. It used to be the section that would be played to make an entire arena of people jump up and down while the music builds and then drops into a section where the bass and the rhythm land hard. The drop can either serve as a post-chorus or, in many cases, replace the chorus. It usually occurs right when you would expect to hear the chorus. The singer may drop out and be replaced with synth sounds and lyrics made up from other lyrics you've heard within the song, or it may just have a repeated tag line, usually the title. This song section should be unique and typically has a beat that is syncopated.

Songs with drop sections:
- "Don't Let Me Down" (the Chainsmokers feat. Daya)
- "Let Me Love You" (DJ Snake feat. Justin Bieber)

TAG

A tag is an irresistible hook line that stays with you after you've heard the song.

Here are two unforgettable tag lines:
- "My Shot" (the musical *Hamilton*) uses *I am not throwing away my shot*.
- "Bad Romance" (Lady Gaga) uses the non-lexical vocables *Rah rah ah-ah-ah*.

It will be up to you to decide how you want to design the form of each song you write. Whether you call a song section a tag, a post-chorus, a drop, or Gary. It doesn't matter as long as it makes your song better.

TRADITIONAL SONG FORMS

- **AAA:** verse/refrain, verse/refrain, verse/refrain
- **AABA:** verse/refrain, verse/refrain, bridge, verse/refrain
- **ABAB:** verse, chorus, verse, chorus
- **ABABCB:** verse, chorus, verse, chorus, bridge, chorus
- **ABCABCDC:** verse, prechorus, chorus, verse, prechorus, chorus, bridge, chorus

HYBRID AND MAVERICK SONG FORMS

- **AABaA:** verse/refrain, verse/refrain, bridge/refrain, verse/refrain
- **AaBAaBCB:** verse/refrain, chorus, verse/refrain, chorus, bridge, chorus
- **ABCDEABCDEFD:** verse, prechorus 1, prechorus 2, chorus, post-chorus; verse, prechorus 1, prechorus 2, chorus, post-chorus, bridge, chorus
- Create your own form.

EXERCISES

1. Write a verse and a chorus.

2. Write a prechorus.

3. Write a post-chorus.

4. Write a tag line hook with non-lexical vocables, like the beginning of Lady Gag's "Bad Romance" or using *ooh, oh,* or *ah.*

5. Invent a new type of song form by creating a unique section.

6. Write a standard verse/refrain song.

ABOUT THE AUTHOR

Photo by Alisa Elliott

Scarlet Keys has been a full-time professor of songwriting at Berklee College of Music since 2003, teaching songwriting, lyric writing, performance, and upper-division songwriting courses. Her former students have included Charlie Puth, Betty Who, Charlie Worsham, Liz Longley, and Jesse Ruben, to name a few.

A former staff songwriter for Warner/Chappell Music, she has released two CDs as a solo artist and toured and performed with her original band.

Her songs have been recorded by other artists spanning the genres of Americana, jazz, country, pop, and folk, both in the United States and in Sweden. Her credits include a gold record, a number 1 song in Britain, and songs placed in film, television, and national commercials. Most recently, she had a song on the *Consenses* CD along with James Taylor, Carly Simon, and Jimmy Buffett, and was a part of the *Consenses* project created by Sally Taylor.

Scarlet has worked and written with Chris Stapleton, Charlie Puth, Melissa Ferrick, Blue Miller of India.Arie, Denny Hemingson of Tim McGraw, hit writer Negin Djafari, Monty Powell, and others.

Scarlet has written articles in *Songwriter's Market* and continues writing and teaching at Berklee and in clinics across the U.S.

INDEX